Stranger Danger

CHARITY CHANDLER-COLE

Ashley, Thank you
for supporting Stranger
Danger! 12/14/23

13TH & JOAN

Stranger Danger. Copyright 2023 by Charity Chandler-Cole. All rights reserved. No part of this publication may be reproduced, distributed, or transmitted in any form or by any means, including photocopying, recording, or other electronic or mechanical methods, without the prior written permission of the publisher, except in the case of brief quotations embodied in critical reviews and certain other noncommercial uses permitted by copyright law.

For permission requests, write to the publisher, addressed "Attention: Permissions Coordinator," 205 N. Michigan Avenue, Suite #810, Chicago, IL 60601. 13th & Joan books may be purchased for educational, business or sales promotional use. For information, please email the Sales Department at sales@13thandjoan.com.

Printed in the U. S. A.

First Printing, July 2023.

Library of Congress Cataloging-in-Publication Data has been applied for.

ISBN: 978-1-961863-29-3

DEDICATION

This book is dedicated to the millions of children who are impacted by the foster care and juvenile justice systems, child sexual exploitation, homelessness, and poverty.

DEAR READER,

WHAT YOU ARE about to read will have you questioning everything and everyone, including yourself.

This book will take you on the ride of a teenage girl whose whole world came crumbling down around her as she became entangled in the web of *Stranger Danger*. She, by default, experienced the extraordinary consequences of our society's deep-rooted hatred, criminalization, and punishment of poverty and race, as well as the entrapment of predators who lied in wait to exploit her vulnerability as a child in the foster care system. Those situated to respond and protect or support her missed opportunity after opportunity to do just that, and instead imposed more harm and trauma that almost led to her demise. Her journey is not unique, but prevalent and in need of attention and action.

I chose to write this book because of my own horrific experience and entanglement with the foster care and juvenile justice systems. The journey you will be reading will be mine according to my personal recollection of events, with other very real stories woven in that highlight the intersectionality of race, poverty, sex, and socioeconomic status. Names have been changed to protect the privacy of others. This ride may be uncomfortable for some and empowering for others, so take a seat and hold on tight. The turbulence gets real.

Warning: Events and issues surrounding this story will be alarming and may be disturbing.

ACKNOWLEDGEMENTS

To my son, Marcus, for giving me
purpose and a reason to live.

To my husband, Terry,
for loving me and being my rock.

TABLE OF CONTENTS

INTRODUCTION

THERE ARE FORCES beyond what we can imagine that exist benevolently under the guise of safety, protection, health, security, and justice. We rely ignorantly on the guidance of individuals in authority, trusting their knowledge and power to lead us in the right direction, to provide answers, solutions, and meaningful experiences. We trust them wholeheartedly with our lives, our bodies, our minds, our secrets, our freedom, our joy, and our children. In reality, they do quite the opposite from our expectations. They steal, they oppress, they criminalize, they punish, they surveille, and they prey. They rely on our ignorance and our trust in them to continue existing and profiting off our oppression and our pain.

We tend to perceive strangers only as individuals we do not know and thereby require caution, observation, distance, and trust before we let down our guards and invite them into our spaces and lives. We do not, however, maintain this same level of scrutiny when these strangers are cloaked and draped in uniforms, badges, and titles that by default let them skip the line and demand our respect and command our submission. These forces are introduced into our lives through individuals who enforce laws, policies, systems, institutions, and structures that were created to control and empower those at the top at the expense of everyone else. These forces are inherently racist and were built from the blood, sweat, and tears of indigenous and enslaved people. These forces stand so tall and strong that they are almost invincible. Seemingly noble and honorable individuals in the form of police officers, teachers, doctors, and social workers—to name a few—are recruited to deliver their message, implement their policies, and perpetuate their oppression. These individuals also take the blame for these forces when accountability and real justice are on the table, while they continue to lurk in the shadows until it's time to strike again. These strangers are the most dangerous.

CHAPTER 1

I T'S JULY 11TH, 2002, and it's a warm day in Los Angeles, California. Our country was bracing for the upcoming one-year anniversary and memorial of 9/11, the day that shook our nation when as many as 3,000 people were killed in a terrorist attack that used hijacked planes to fly into the twin towers of the World Trade Center in New York and the Pentagon. My grandma died that day too, but not from the attacks. Her cigarette smoking finally caught up to her and lung cancer paid her a foreseeable visit.

While millions and billions of dollars were being spent to fight terrorism abroad, our very real and ignored societal and psychological wars domestically had me sitting in the backseat of an LAPD police car, terrified and headed to juvenile hall. My dumb ass got caught stealing underwear from the Ross Dress for Less on 3rd and Fairfax, across the street from the infamous Grove where all the who's who and well-off white people went to shop and dine. There was the occasional sprinkle of Asians, Blacks and Hispanics, many of whom were enjoying the outdoor ambiance and window shopping or being indulged by an older white man. These men traded high-end designer gifts for companionship and fake interest in their dull, lonely, and pathetic life that they disguised in designer suits, 6,500-square-foot homes in Beverly Hills, and foreign cars.

Don't get me wrong, I wasn't dumb for stealing the underwear. I needed those and I promised my little sister that I would get her some. I was dumb because I successfully got out of the store without getting caught, and went back looking for my friend, Brittany, who should have been right behind me. We had a rule: You get out and you don't look back. If you lose each other, which often happens, you meet back up at a specific location or see each other the next day at school where we would laugh and joke about how ridiculous we looked in our oversized coats in the dead of summer, or any new tactics we used to give the appearance of innocence. On this day in particular, it was my one-year anniversary with my boyfriend at the time, Joseph, and we had plans to hang out after my quick Ross errand, so I was annoyed that I had to waste precious time going back to look for her. What I thought would have been a quick, *"Bitch, hurry up,"* turned into me getting grabbed by two Loss Prevention wannabe top-flight security officers. I was escorted into a back room where Brittany was waiting, scared out of her mind and crying uncontrollably.

Brittany was a ward of the court, a kid in foster care who was living with her mean-ass auntie who had a daughter a few years younger than her who she treated like royalty. I always compared Brittany's situation to a real-life Cinderella story, minus the prince, fairy godmother, and happy ending. Brittany's aunt got a monthly check for her, so she put up with her, gave her the bare minimum, and made sure to remind her of how generous she was, and how lucky Brittany was to not be living in a foster home.

Brittany is what we would call a redbone, a light-skinned Black girl, with black curly hair that would be frizzy and uncontrollable one day and slick and bouncy the next day. It was like her hair, much like herself, was fighting a dual consciousness each day of either embracing the Black and whiteness that ran in its genes and DNA, or resisting the parts of it that weren't socially acceptable.

Because our society, and even our community, valued whiteness over darkness and gave preference to the proximity of lightness, redbones were seen as more desirable over dark-skinned girls. Colorism was a real thing in our community. Whether it was through TV shows like *Martin,* where you had redbone Gina setting the tone for what actresses should look like, or the lead singers of our favorite girl groups like Destiny's Child, where Beyonce was the star, front and center and leading all of the songs, lightness or anything white adjacent was cultivated in our minds and our world as being superior and better than. So, imagine Brittany, in all her light-skinned glory, being saved from the grips of foster care by her very dark-skinned and nappy-haired aunt and cousin.

While the world glorified her lightness, other Black women and Black girls detested her for it. They didn't detest her beauty, lightness, and glistening hair. They detested how society compared their darkness to hers, how others made them feel ashamed of the skin they were born with and inferior to her, and how they felt the need to constantly compete with the very women they should be loving and embracing. Brittany's aunt made sure that her dark-skinned daughter was the one exalted in her home. It was her prerogative that her daughter's Black-girl magic was not overshadowed and on full display at all times, and that the treatment Brittany received would be practice for how her daughter would handle the cruel world that was waiting to shred her dignity and humanity to pieces, simply because of the amount of melanin in her skin. Brittany wasn't sure why her aunt was so mean to her, nor was she grateful to be living with her. She just tried to not get in trouble too often because she didn't want to upset her aunt, but she yearned to fit in and be accepted in her neighborhood. Like me, she did what she needed to survive.

Poverty was real and our neighborhood was unforgiving. We were all pretty poor at the end of the day, but there were levels to poverty. If you were too far down on the totem pole, or at least gave that appearance, it became open season. You would become the target of mean and cruel kids using you as the verbal and physical punching bag that helped them feel a little better about their own situations.

I met Brittany in front of Shenandoah Elementary School in West LA while we waited for our school bus to take us to Mark Twain Middle School in Venice, which was the nearest public middle school. She immediately recognized the new kids walking up, me the 8th-grader and my little sister, Harmony, the 6th-grader. Brittany was in the 7th grade and desperate for friends. Her best bet was to recruit us before any other girls did, and it worked. We didn't know at the time that Brittany was the kid who would always get bullied by other girls and was the target of most of all the darker-skinned Black girls. She presented herself as a cool kid, offered to show us around and help us get acclimated, and of course let us know who all the cute boys were, which ones were already taken, and which ones to watch out for. She had an anxious confidence about herself, like she was acting and playing a role she didn't fully embrace. She turned up the acting when around us and would simmer down when she was around other people, especially other girls at our school. It was like her light was immediately dimmed in certain spaces. I was happy to have her embrace us on our first day of school, and we immediately made Brittany our play cousin and became pretty protective of her.

Being the mahogany-skinned tone girls that we were, but definitely feeling the full brunt of being Black, we were accepted by both the dark-skinned and the light-skinned girls. I think Brittany thought she could use us as her way in. My sister and I had each other. We were tough and were always ready to check anyone who came at us sideways. I guess that's what happens when your parents have four daughters back-to-back. We fought each other just as hard as we loved each other, and would quickly check anyone that stepped to one of our siblings incorrectly, so much so that we started our first clique in middle school called *Letting Bitches Have It,* or *LBH*. We mainly just hung out and stuck together during lunch with our new friends. There were about 11 of us. We had double Dutch competitions that would end in a lot of shit talking and of course, meeting for our own little drill team practice after school once our bus dropped us back off at Shenandoah. We would always have a good 30 minutes before it was time to pick up our younger siblings from the after-school program and walk them home. Our bond with Brittany grew strong during middle school. She was our friend and our sister, but despite having us and joining our little clique, she was still weak and fake as hell. I imagine that had to do with what she was dealing with at home. Fake empowered and strong at school, and mental and emotional degradation at home.

Fast forward to now, a few years later and in the grip of these trifling-ass security guards. They were both Hispanic, in their late 20s, or early 30s, and both too damn excited with their catch, like they got points or commission for catching people stealing. Heck, maybe they did. I'm sure the white store owners made them feel real good about going above and beyond to protect their property, white property, which in our society had more value than Black life. In any case, they took their job way too seriously to be getting only minimum wage, and I was ready to get out of there, like ASAP. I looked around the room that was painted in a dingy blueish gray and quickly noticed a collage of pictures posted on the wall of previous transgressors who were no longer allowed in the store. I wasn't too worried about making the wall of shame because this Ross location was kinda far anyway. I could definitely live without walking miles to come here when I had one by my house off of Sawyer and LaCienega.

"Sir," (asshole in my head), "what's the plan? We're sorry for stealing, we won't do it again. Can we go?" I asked.

Because we were minors, they had to call our parents to pick us up from the store. I guess since it was petty theft, our consequence was whatever our parents imposed on us for having to get the embarrassing call and waste precious gas to pick us up—not to mention having to leave work early, which in our community meant lost wages and an excuse for your racist, intolerant boss to fire you for having a family emergency. Rent-a-Cop #1 called Brittany's aunt first, who picked up the phone on the first ring. You could hear Brittany's aunt hissing through the phone, pissed that she had to get up off the couch from watching her soaps to pick her up.

"Can't she just walk home? I don't have time for this shit!" Brittany's aunt shouted through the phone. Rent-a-Cop #1 explained that she needed to sign something, so her presence was required.

"This some bullshit, I'm on my way." Click.

After being hung up on by Brittany's aunt, you could tell how annoyed he was, and even a bit disgusted by the angry Black woman who had the nerve to hang up in his face. He began to dial my mother's number next and braced himself for what he assumed to be another angry Black-woman call.

I gave Brittany a slick smile, assuring her that everything would be alright and we'd survive the long-ass lectures and insults we'd get that night. While trying to reach my mom, the phone rang and rang. After one hopeless attempt, Rent-a-Cop #1 tried a second time. I got a little anxious knowing my mom was at work and couldn't really answer the phone. She had just gotten a job through the CalWorks welfare-to-work program and was hired by the Federal Aviation Administration (FAA), who were participating in the program to help poor people like us by offering mothers on welfare entry-level jobs. It started off as a temporary position, but was a huge deal for my mom who just overcame a nasty divorce and her battle with breast cancer. Between this job and getting a three-bedroom apartment through Section 8, things were finally starting to look a little normal for her and the last thing she needed was one of her six kids fucking it up.

She finally answered after the second try, and all I could hear after Rent-a-Cop #1 said, *"we'll have to call the police if no one comes,"* was her growling in the loudest whisper-like tone, *"Call the police, hell, take her to jail! Let them deal with it!"*

My jaw dropped immediately and the two asshole Rent-a-Cop's busted up laughing, thinking she was playing, but she wasn't. Their expressions quickly changed from humor back to business as I ran to the phone asking to speak with her, but she refused and hung up the phone. What the fuck! How could she say that? How dare she hang up without speaking to me? I was livid. I quickly looked over at Brittany who was just as shocked as I was and as wide-eyed as a deer in headlights. I didn't know what to think, but I just knew there was no way in hell they would take me to jail for stealing underwear. I was only 16 years old, so she HAD to come get me, right? The Rent-a-Cops were used to calling the police on people, so they proceeded with their call telling the police station they had a kid that needed to be picked up for theft. What the hell.

"Can't I just leave with Brittany when her aunt comes? Are you seriously calling the police right now?!" I asked.

The bullshit ass Rent-a-Cops said it was out of their control and I shouldn't have been stealing anyway, so this is the risk I took. I immediately became anxious and nervous and stared at the door we came through looking to see if there was any possible way for me to make a run for it. This could not be happening. Why didn't I just keep going instead of coming back for Brittany? This was her idea anyway to come way down here to this stupid-ass Ross, which clearly had more ambitious security and a keen eye for poor Black kids who stood out in this community—a community their asses weren't even from either.

Brittany swore they had better shit here because they catered to a more affluent community, and she was right. We found Coach shoes, Girbaud, Karl Kani, and even DKNY up here. Granted, our Ross definitely carried the brands we liked such as Fubu, Pepe, Pelle Pelle, Phat Farm, and Ecko. In any case, Brittany was looking for something a little fancier than the hood apparel we proudly doused, so here we were, stealing because we definitely couldn't afford none of this shit, not even from a discount store like Ross. Some days we stole food and clothes out of pure necessity and hunger, and other days we stole as a means of protection. If our clothes weren't dingy and had a little name brand that was trending, we were safe from the other kids who would walk around like cheesy hyenas, preying on poor, unfortunate souls. It's roast or be roasted, and we'd take predator over prey any day. Kids didn't think about the harm and trauma they were causing other kids. We were too young to fully grasp that, and too much in survival mode to really give a damn. We could only see and feel our pain. We lived in our experience and ours alone. It drove us to do all kinds of things to fit in and feel accepted, from smoking weed to selling drugs, stealing, and beating another kid's ass from time to time simply because they looked at you. This is the world we lived in. This is the childhood we had to survive.

My mother didn't give a damn about any of that though, or at least we couldn't tell she did. She had her own shit she was trying to survive. It's been over five years since she divorced my father, the man she fell for when she left

11

Baltimore to come to Los Angeles to be an actress, singer, and model. She believed Hollywood was the answer to her dreams, the way out of her crappy reality and her path to success, opportunity, and if she's lucky, even fame and fortune, if she could only make it there. She made it here all right, but instead of having a thriving career in entertainment, she became a deacon's wife, converted from Catholicism to Christianity, and found herself pregnant for eight-and-a-half years straight, giving life to my five siblings and me.

Instead of modeling couture down glamorous walkways during fashion week, or singing opera at the renowned Ahmanson Theater, she found herself wobbling down grocery store aisles with a big belly and swollen ankles to stack cans of tuna, or standing for hours to scan item after item and greet customers with a mandated smile at the Vons checkout lane. She resented my father for thwarting her dream. It was all she ever really wanted. Instead, she escaped one bad situation and landed in another. She thought it was love, she wanted to be loved by him, this charming 5'8" man with the most beautiful curly hair she'd ever seen on a Black man that he often picked out into an afro. He had a slender frame that made him appear a little taller than he actually was, a smooth smile that would part to reveal the most beautiful teeth, and when he spoke, he oozed brilliance and confidence. This young man of only 25 years had game, so much so that she was willing to delay, or even cancel her dream of fame and fortune to follow him as his faithful believer, lover, and wife.

He convinced her that he was a prophet, that God had his hand on him and that if she believed, if she trusted him and obeyed the word and command of the Lord, that she would be blessed and highly favored. Her new-found devotion and belief in God brought her happiness. When she gave her life to God and committed to His word, she felt a presence overtake her that felt like a blanket of peace and love. She clung to this feeling like a dope fiend to a pipe and would do whatever it took to keep that feeling alive, even following all of my father's orders and demands as instructed by the Bible. Instead of giving herself to the world to be idolized and sexualized as a model, she found a way to use her many gifts and talents in the church choir as a passionate soprano, and on the praise dance team where she really felt one with God and intertwined in His glory. Praying, singing, and dancing gave my mom solace. It was her escape and her reason for pressing on in her terrible marriage.

My father was a narcissist who was never satisfied. She couldn't do anything right. She couldn't cook right, couldn't clean right, and damn sure couldn't conceive children right. My father wanted sons, but with each pregnancy came a girl, then another, and another, and another. With each back-to-back pregnancy my mother got fatter, sadder, and less desirable by my father, and he made sure she knew it. She wanted to give him a boy. She told herself if she did, he would love her again, they'd be happy once more like they were before she said *"I do"* and he revealed his true colors. So, she kept having his babies. She needed the boy just as much as he did, her baby boy would be her golden ticket and everything would be alright. She convinced herself that the fighting would stop, the insults would cease, she'd be happy again, the weight from all the stress and depression and breeding would start to melt away. All of the running after her rambunctious daughters who were just as tough as little boys, the sleepless nights, nonstop breastfeeding and days on her feet at the grocery store while carrying them all in her womb would have been worth it. When baby number five arrived, the golden, coveted boy was born with another boy following immediately after by accident. To her dismay, nothing changed and after another five years of suffering my father's verbal and emotional abuse, she left him.

I don't recall what I felt when we learned they would be divorcing, probably relief. Don't get me wrong, my father was a great dad, although he was strict and had a paddle he would whoop us with called Mr. No Games until our behinds were numb- he loved us dearly, all of us. I felt relief because my parents argued everyday and it was exhausting to hear and watch. I couldn't tell you what they were even arguing about most of the time. The times I do recall were over the house not being as clean as he would like. My father expected my mother to not only work full time like he did, but also take care of the six of us, keep the house clean, and have dinner waiting for him when he walked through the door. Patriarchy was real in our home. There was a clear order to things and us girls were not exempt from it.

I can only vividly recall my parents being happy one time. It was bedtime, and I heard smooth jazz playing downstairs. We'd normally only hear gospel music playing in the house which meant my mother was either cleaning, maybe cooking, or dancing around praising the Lord. My dad was the one who listened to jazz, and he only listened to it in his car on 94.7 The Wave. So to hear it playing in the house was odd, and my curiosity peaked. I got out of my bed and quietly tiptoed to the top of the staircase. It would be my ass if I got caught out of bed, but I needed to know what was going on down there. At the top of the stairs, I laid down on my stomach and started to slide down head first, just enough to peek through the first spindle of the staircase to see down into the kitchen. To my surprise, my father was holding my mother in his arms and together they swayed side to side to the tune of the jazz vinyl playing on the turntable my mother found at a yard sale and gifted to my father. They looked happy and at peace, almost like they loved each other. My mother seemed content as she closed her eyes and smiled as the joy of the moment engulfed her and the sound of the music serenaded her. Was this what love looked like on display? I could get used to this and wanted badly to get up, run down the stairs, and insert myself between them while they danced. I wanted to feel their love at the same time, look up and see their kind eyes and happy smiles gazing down on me, showering me with the rays of joy I felt escaping their warm bodies. I lost myself in this thought and found that I had started daydreaming when the loud stomping frightened me out of my blissful moment. I quietly jumped up and ran to my room. I don't know what was said as they held each other tightly, but something clearly upset my father and disappointed my mother and ruined the single memory I would have of a seemingly loving and healthy relationship.

By the time I turned 10, my parents would be divorced and my mother fighting an incredible battle of stage 4 breast cancer that the doctors assured us would take her life in less than a year. By some miracle, or as my mom would say,

"God's grace," she lived another 20 years and the only thing she lost was her left breast, her once well-behaved children, and her goddong mind. The chemo and drugs coupled with her childhood trauma, emotional marital abuse, and believing she would die and leave her six children behind did a number on her mental health. She was never diagnosed with anything at the time, but she was clearly not the same person anymore. Now a single mom taking care of six kids on her own without any support from my father and trying her best to survive and provide for us, she slowly started to give up. It was too much for her. We were too much for her. So at just 16 years old, there I was, being given up on by my mother who was physically, mentally and emotionally exhausted with the life she was dealt and the responsibilities that came with it.

When I was greeted by the two police officers upon their arrival to the store, they spoke briefly with the two Rent-a-Cops who were awfully proud to engage with the police and present their catch of the day. It was almost disgusting to watch them act like happy puppies that were being patted on the head and given the treat of acknowledgement in the only scenario where their brown bodies would be seen as an ally and not a foe. The two officers looked at me, asked me to stand up and turn around, put my hands behind my back and proceeded to place cold handcuffs on me. With each click of the tightening of the cuffs, I held my breath hoping my skin wouldn't get caught in them like I saw on a TV show. They also didn't read me any Miranda Rights like they did on the show, so I figured those parts were just made up for TV.

After being handcuffed, I was escorted through the store and everyone who was shopping stopped to watch. I immediately felt a blanket of shame and embarrassment, and lowered my head in an unsuccessful attempt to hide from the glaring eyes and looks of disgust on the bystanders' faces. I wondered what they thought I did to justify this public performance and shaming. The two police officers didn't speak to me at all. They didn't ask me why I was stealing. They were not accompanied by a social worker who would ask all the right questions and ask my mother, ultimately, why she wouldn't or couldn't come get me—or better yet, why her daughter was stealing underwear for her little sister. No one lectured me or told me there were other ways to get clothing and support to address the poverty my family was experiencing outside of stealing. Zero questions were asked and zero fucks were given. My actions and my arrest were viewed as normal and acceptable in everyone's eyes. I was the only one who was completely shocked by what I perceived to be a societal atrocity.

The drive to the LAPD Wilshire Division Police Station seemed incredibly long to be only less than 10 minutes away. The uncomfortable, hard plastic seats and being handcuffed with my arms behind my back made the trip almost unbearable. Any wrong move or bump in the ground would cause the handcuffs to bang against the hard seat and my shoulder to jerk in a way that left a paralyzing discomfort. I didn't understand why I needed to be handcuffed. I stuffed panties and an orange Rocawear t-shirt in my pants. I didn't stick the place up with a Smith & Wesson.

The handcuffs, public shaming, and paralyzing ride to the police station were nothing compared to the treatment I received during booking. I felt like I was watching an episode of *Law and Order* as adult vagrants were being brought in, cursing and shouting, or in some cases, completely high and unaware that they were even in a police station being hauled in and away for darkening the door steps of business establishments that saw their homelessness and begging as a crime. There were women and girls caged inside holding cells who were wearing outfits that left nothing to the imagination, whose crime was soliciting sex in exchange for money they would later use to pay rent, buy groceries for their children, or reluctantly have to turn over to a pimp that lured them in with the promise of protection and support, but failed to mention the black eyes, exploitation, and mental and physical kidnapping they'd experience.

I was led to a counter where I was asked to give my name, address, and date of birth. There was no reaction to my being 16 years old and being brought to this vile and depressing place. I was then taken to a wall to have my picture taken, or as it is infamously known, my mug shot. First staring forward, then the left side, then the right. I surprisingly wasn't given a sign to hang around my neck like John Lewis had, or a number to hold like the one I saw of Rosa Parks. Just a photo session that resulted in a picture that bore the face of a scared little girl that was in for a rude awakening. I was asked next to take the shoestrings out of my shoes, take off my belt, and remove the hair ties from my hair. All of my other belongings had already been taken. I was later told that my shoestrings were removed so that I didn't try to hang myself with them. I couldn't imagine why I would do such a thing, but it all made sense later. I was processed, booked, and awaiting transport to Eastlake Central Juvenile Hall.

CHAPTER 2

WHEN I ARRIVED at Eastlake Juvenile Hall, I had no idea what to expect. I didn't have time to imagine the layout or what the sleeping arrangements would be. I didn't think about how many other kids would be there, what the food would taste like, or the daily routine. My mind was racing, undoubtedly, but I was still trying to understand how I could be handcuffed and sent to jail for what they termed petty theft. Hopping out of the bare, white van with deep tinted windows and CA EXEMPT license plates that picked me up from the police precinct, I stared up in complete terror at the place I would be calling home for God knows how long. The building was massive and stretched as far as I could see. As my eyes slowly climbed the cracked and peeling cream-colored wall, they froze at the sight of the sharp barbed wire that lined the top of every wall. I gulped, terrified of what awaited me on the other side of those walls. Clearly, they were trying to keep horrific people that could scale a wall four times their height from leaving, which really made me question why I was here.

I moved quickly through a gate that required an officer on the other side to buzz us in, then a metal door whose thick bolted locks snapped back and screeched open, granting us access. We were greeted by a correctional officer, or CO as they liked to be called, who exchanged a few brief words and laughs with my handler, enjoying the quick catch up before leaving me to collect the next kid who warranted a transport to this God-awful place. The CO was tall, Black, and wore a French roll hairstyle that reminded me of the time my mom got her hair done real nice by her friend at the cosmetology school. She looked at the paper my handler gave her and said, *"You Chandler?"*

"Yes," I replied, or at least I thought I did, but the words were trapped in the deep gulp I took on the way in. *"Are you Charity Chandler?"*

"Ye...ss," I managed to stutter. *"Date of birth?"*

"05/25/1986," I replied. After confirming I was indeed the person on her paper, I was instructed to take off my clothes—panties, bra, everything. I slowly peeled them off, one layer at a time. With each piece of clothing removed, I could feel the chill bumps forming over my body from the cold of the room. I became more and more self-conscious of my body and how vulnerable and powerless I was in that moment. Looking around, the room was completely bare, with just a purple plastic chair, cold concrete floors, and windowless walls. Stepping out of my blue denim jeans, I was grateful for the black oversized ProClub T-shirt I wore to stuff stolen items into, because it now served as a dress that provided a brief moment of cover for the parts of me I thought I had control over. I paused while holding the base of my shirt, a fist full in each hand, and flashed back to the one other time this act caused me the level of anxiety and pressure I was feeling now.

I was 14 and in my boyfriend's bedroom. I met him in the eighth grade while attending Mark Twain Middle School in Venice, California. He was a tall, beautiful boy. Light-skinned, green eyes, cornrows, and big lips that parted to show the most mischievous smile and alluring gap. His frame and posture radiated confidence and strength, and he appeared to be much older than an eighth-grader. All of the girls at our school were in love with this kid, but for some reason I was the one that caught his eye and warranted his attention. Out of all the girls, I was the one that wasn't giving him the time of day, or was impressed with all of the game he thought he had. I actually enjoyed laughing at all of the ridiculous things that came out of his mouth and watching how gullible all the girls were, including my friends. He was attracted to me simply because I wasn't attracted to him. The hunt was on, and while I entertained the chase, I had no idea how this boy would change my life. Eventually his smooth talking and walking me and my siblings home everyday from the bus stop paid off, and I accepted the offer to become his girlfriend. With him I experienced my first real intimate and passionate kiss. I allowed him to touch me in places that only I had touched, and I allowed him to convince me that he owned me because I was his girlfriend. I had real daddy issues at this point and absolutely no adult guidance, role models, or mentors. Because I didn't want to lose the feeling of protection, warmth, and the consistent presence that came with being his girl and that I lacked from my own father, coupled with the fear of what would happen if I objected, I was afraid to say no. I didn't know I could say no without consequence. The one time I did, it earned me a busted lip and me being face down on the cold pavement with his knee in my back, while my little sister and other kids in the neighborhood watched me be humiliated by the beloved green-eyed boy.

I learned early on in our relationship that he was in control. While I thought that control protected me from the harshness of the outside world, it scared the hell out of me. He made it clear that I belonged to him and there was no escaping our relationship. He owned me, and when he felt it was time to bring our intimacy to a new level, I feared what would happen if I said no. I knew I wasn't ready, but I didn't have a choice. I was scared. But he, being the virgin he was also, was ready to prove to his boys that he could get it. His friends, who were probably virgins themselves, mocked and joked about him being a virgin and how lame he was because he had a girlfriend and wasn't getting any. He was adamant about proving them wrong and demanded that we had sex, immediately. So there I was, being told to undress with two fists full of my t-shirt as I whipped it off over my head and laid down slowly on my back.

While I waited for him to get undressed and climb on top of me, I felt my palms start to sweat and I contemplated what, if anything, I could say to get out of this. But absolutely nothing came to mind. Now on top of me, I could feel the weight of his body and the weight of the peer-pressure he was feeling as he worked his way inside of me. I took in a deep pull of air and held my breath. I never felt pain like that before. It was as if someone took a large round object and launched it into my tiny body, burrowing deeper and deeper, similar to what I would imagine a groundhog or prairie dog does, until I felt it at the pit of my stomach. Then repeat, over and over again. As I tried to muffle the shriek of complete terror I felt, I witnessed the pleasure and euphoria he was experiencing as he was taking his first steps, or strokes, into manhood. Within those two debilitating minutes, he had arrived, at the expense of my innocence. When I started bleeding, I thought he had broken me. My parents didn't prepare me for this moment. We hadn't talked about the birds and the bees or, if I had to describe it, the cherries and bananas. I had no clue what this moment meant for my 14-year-old body. I had no idea the risks I was taking, the protection I needed, the rights I had. All I knew was that I couldn't say no and when I could no longer take the pain and asked him to stop, he refused. I was weak and powerless. What happened to the girl that was *letting bitches have it*? The girl who was strong, confident and a leader amongst her peers? All the facade I put on at school quickly faded, and I was confronted at the intersection of peer pressure, puppy love, security, pain, and terror. I was at my weakest and this low point for me was the high he needed to transcend and elevate his status in the little social world we relied on for our legitimacy in this world. That moment made it clear that my body was not my own and that there were powers greater than mine that could cause a sense of insecurity and vulnerability that are indescribable.

So, there I stood in the cold gray room, inside the juvenile hall with two fists full of my Pro Club T-shirt, preparing to whip it over my head, just like I had been instructed to do before. I took a deep breath, sighed, and prepared for the fucking of my life.

After undressing and standing nude with my arms awkwardly crossed over my breast and vagina in the most desperate attempt to cover both for what seemed like forever, the CO finally handed me a pair of underwear that bore menstrual cycle stains that clearly couldn't be washed out, an oversized light gray T-shirt, and dingy navy-blue pants that were turning gray from being washed what looked like 100 times. These clothes had previously covered the bodies of dozens, if not hundreds, of kids before reaching me. If these clothes could talk, I wonder what they would say. Would they recount the fear and anxiety I was feeling at that moment? Would these clothes reveal the pain and tears of kids that tried their best to wipe them away into the stiff fabric? They would probably recall the terrifying days when young girls got their first periods and were all alone and unsure what to do with the panties they had now soiled, not knowing that their mark would live on until the next girl had to wear them. I would soon also feel the agony of expecting teen mothers who were either trying their best to hide their pregnancy, or recovering from vomiting over a cold metal toilet as they grappled with the reality they were now faced with. These clothes would definitely speak of the night sweats that left them dripping wet as kids squared off with the most horrific and terrifying dreams that tormented them and forced them to relive their trauma. I wondered what stories these clothes would one day tell of me, and the journey I had only just begun to embark on.

Anxious to cover my body, I put on the uniform of the detained, incarcerated youth that symbolized my punishment and criminalization quicker than a poor kid getting their first pair of coveted Jordan's. I was then handed a pair of dingy socks and lace-less shoes that reminded me of the vans I once begged my mother for, except these were not branded with the famous logo. I found it odd that I was never asked what size shoes and clothes I wore. The shoes were at least a whole size too small and my prisoner uniform was definitely two sizes too big. I didn't bother saying anything. I had a feeling that I didn't have any rights in this place, and the COs definitely didn't give me the impression of showing any concern or care for how well my clothing fit. I was lastly handed a thin, coarse blanket that felt like sandpaper and told this would be the only one I got, so I better not lose it. My hair was messy and unkempt after having my hair ties removed at the police station, and my edges sweaty and coiled after navigating the stress of the situation, the hot muggy van ride and congested ventless corridors of the jail. I felt ugly, ashamed, and demeaned while the CO stared at me, void of emotion, smacking her gum loudly, and watching my every move. Seeing that I was dressed, she knocked two times on the windowless, metal door and screamed *"READY."* Within an instant, another CO came into the room to collect me, this one a tall and stocky Mexican woman with red dyed hair that she pulled back into a ponytail. She looked at me for maybe half a second. She didn't care why I was there and wasn't interested in speaking to me. She had a job to do, and collecting me was just as transactional as a grocery store cashier scanning a food item and sliding it to the left before reaching for the next item on the belt. So, blanket in arms, I stepped out to follow her, no longer as my first name, Charity, but as inmate Chandler.

CHAPTER 3

I WALKED OUT THE door, through a metal detector, and then another set of locked metal doors, arriving eventually outside to a vast open space within the secured walls of the juvenile hall. There were two-story buildings, some one-story, and grass that had blotches of green, but mainly yellow and dry ground with a few bare patches, dirt mounds and concrete. I spied another CO walking toward us with a line of about six teenage boys trailing behind him, their arms behind their backs and hands all forming the shape of a diamond. Behind them was another CO, I imagined to ensure no one fell out of line, or their place. Seeing me, the boys stared hard, some smiling with mischievous grins that were hiding their own fears and pain; one licking his lips as if I was being served to them on a platter; and another just a blank stare, his eyes deep, lost and void, almost as if he was just drifting by with no purpose or existence. I quickly glanced away, still ashamed and embarrassed by my appearance, hoping to never see or be remembered by them again.

It had only been two years since my body started developing and resembling features of a young woman. I was a part of the itty-bitty titty committee (IBTC) all through middle school, while many of my friends' bosoms started to blossom and made a point to show off their new bras. My boobs didn't come until the summer after 8th grade graduation, but right before starting high school. Despite moving on from the IBTC, I didn't realize I was actually somewhat cute until the 10th grade when I got kicked out of Hamilton High and had to go to Westchester High. Westchester was totally different from Hami, and kids made a point of showing up and showing off whatever fashion, designer clothes and fresh kicks they had. Having very little to none myself, I got by on the fact that people thought I was pretty, and apparently had "good hair" according to them, and the beauty standards dictated by the media and society at large. That gave me a few extra points and helped take away from the fact that I mainly only wore chucks and keds everyday and the most basic of outfits that I could switch up and duplicate without too many people noticing. One of my friends, Charlene, would come to school everyday with a full face of makeup on, hair on point and looking like a tall, dark, beautiful, ebony model that should have been gracing the cover of a magazine. I started to get into eye liner, lip liner, gloss, and occasionally mascara to amplify my beauty and help continue to take away from the fact that my gear was pretty weak compared to the other kids. This awareness and vanity I now had was fairly new, so being seen in such a despicable situation and looking like I was picked up off the streets for vagrancy was extremely humiliating and quickly diminished any self-confidence I had only recently acquired. Maybe that too, was a part of my punishment.

As we walked toward the girls' unit, I was totally unprepared for what came next. As soon as the door opened and we walked in, I could hear one of the COs yelling, *"Johnson, sit your ass down, right now,"* to a Black detained girl who was no taller than 4'11, maybe 80 pounds and wore her hair up in a ponytail that was secured with multiple layers of toilet paper that was tightly twisted together to form a hair tie. *"Bitch, I'll beat yo ass, you fucking beaner,"* Johnson yelled, completely ignoring the CO's demands to stop and with her eyes laser focused on another detained girl, Recinos, who was physically being held back by another CO. I assumed Recinos was Mexican, a mistake I later learned led to real social consequences because all Spanish speaking people were not Mexican, which is what I thought growing up. Breaking loose, which was easy to do with her tiny, short frame, Johnson darted over to Recinos faster than the Tasmanian devil from Looney Tunes. Swinging her arm back as far as she could, Johnson launched it forward, throwing a hard blow that landed square in Recinos' face, sending all 170 lbs of her 5'3" and stocky frame crashing into the metal table she was sitting on. Johnson proceeded to straddle Recinos and threw blow after blow, blood now oozing from her nose. I was amazed that this little girl, who was definitely no older than 14 or 15 years old, had the courage and audacity to fully put on display that her bite was just as big as her bark and that she wasn't afraid of *"no big-ass, sweaty bitch,"* as she boldly exclaimed. Johnson's friends stood nearby laughing and egging her on, giving her the affirmation she needed to keep beating Recinos' ass until the COs were finally able to break up the fight. The unit, now filled with shouting, tension, chaos, and pissed-off adults, was immediately put on lockdown, and I was shoved into what would be my new bedroom.

I stood frozen in my tiny cell. This was definitely not quite the introduction and tour of my new living quarters that I was expecting. Although, I'm not sure exactly what I was expecting. Sometimes, parents in my neighborhood would threaten to call the cops on their little kids if they were bad, sending them into an immediate crying episode, followed by promises that they'd be good. A tactic that moreso derived from the known treatment and abuse of Black folk by police and carceral systems, than the idea of being housed in a concrete jungle itself. There also weren't any shows on TV that showed kids locked up. Although we would sometimes hear about some of the kids in our neighborhood going to juvie, we never really received any details about the experience, like what it looked or felt like. We only got the exaggerated stories that made our homies coming out of jail look like glorified bad-asses who survived a trip to the pen, as we called it, and as a result were rewarded additional hood credit that they wore as a badge of honor.

While processing the flood of emotions that were beginning to pour down on me like a torrential rain, I slowly started to look around and feel the tiny space closing in on me. My bed was a piece of concrete that projected from a white, heavily stained concrete wall, defaced with words and drawings that vividly articulated the thoughts, feelings, and emotions of past children who inhabited the space. Teardrops, single eye balls lightly drawn by a piece of lead removed from a pencil, or lines drawn with blood from a pricked finger forming a sad face decorated my walls. On top of my concrete bed was a green removable padding that was no thicker than two yoga mats stacked on top of each other and a pillow made of rough plastic, easy for cleaning I suppose. Next to the bed was a stainless-steel toilet bowl and small stainless-steel sink that I would learn that night came with a loud leak that would echo through my cell and prevent me from fully escaping this nightmare by succumbing to what I prayed would be a peaceful slumber. The floor was gray concrete and cold. I took two steps toward the door to peer through the sliver of a window and only see other dingy metal doors that were closed and locked, housing the powerless and scared soul of another girl that our society has cast aside. Stepping back and now sitting on my bed, back against the cold wall and knees bent up high enough for me to tuck my face into, I let the full weight of my emotions take over and I cried a deep cry I never cried before.

The shock of my experience had worn off and I was beginning to feel the un-numbing effect of what was happening to me. I was in jail, locked up, and completely uncertain of what lay ahead for me. I couldn't stop crying, I lost all control. At that moment, I wanted my mom. I wanted to beg for her forgiveness and for her to stop everything and come get me. I wanted someone, anyone, to hear my cries and come rescue me and tell me it was going to be ok. All I got was a loud banging on the door and being told to, "Quiet it down, Chandler." Grabbing my sandpaper blanket, I shoved it into my mouth to muffle my sobbing. I couldn't stop crying, no matter how hard I tried. By the time a CO finally came to my door what had to be hours later, I was so congested from crying that I could barely breathe. My face was soiled and flustered, with visible veins protruding through my forehead, just like the varicose veins on my elementary school librarian's calves. It was time for dinner and my first real introduction to my cell mates. Based on what I witnessed so far, I was scared...real scared.

I never considered myself a tough girl, rough girl, or a mean girl. I did tough, rough, and mean things on occasion, but it was always out of a need to survive. Deep down inside I was a girl who loved to read, was very kind and generous and if I had things my way, would spend every waking second exploring libraries, museums, and nature. I would often bury my head in a book and escape to a far-away land that gave me a sense of solace and refuge from the poverty-stricken reality I was living. Every tough situation I found myself in was a matter of survival. I either had to defend myself, or my siblings, or engage in less socially acceptable behavior, like stealing clothes and food, or selling nickel bags of marijuana to help make up for the gap that was left after my mother cashed her paycheck. Ninth grade was a real reality check for me. The Payless shoes that tormented my elementary school years and the pair of Saucony's I got in middle school after the church took up an offering for my family when they thought my mom was going to die of breast cancer, were no longer cutting it in high school. At that point, I had switched from our little middle-school clique to a real gang, and not because I wanted to, but because I knew I had to. My younger siblings' safety and protection relied on it, plus it was seen as a rite of passage in our neighborhood.

I was introduced to selling weed right when the ninth grade started. Normally, my friends and I would hang out at our big homie's house and smoke their weed, drink their liquor, and giggle whenever we could hear real adult activities happening in the next room. One day after school, we were walking home and met up with some of our big homies who we were walking back to their apartment from the corner store. As we were walking, we hear "SHOOO WOOP," which was a term we used to alert the hood that Five-O, or the police, were on the block. Caesar, who was the only Mexican from our hood and held one of the coveted titles of "big homie," stood 6'3" and had the body of a linebacker. He immediately took a Glock out of his waist and three dub sacks of chronic—the good weed—from his pocket. He told me to put it in my backpack, walk on the other side of the street, and act like I didn't know any of them. I could see the police car in the distance hurrying down the block, so without even questioning or thinking twice, I did as I was told. I looked on from across the street, watching and walking as my friends were pulled up on by the police, frisked, and sat on a curb with their arms handcuffed behind their backs.

Within an instant, I went from being perceived as just the home girl, to a loyal member of the crew. Apparently, they knew something I didn't, which was that the police wouldn't bother to look across the street at the innocent 14-year-old girl who was walking home from school with a Jansport backpack. They were there for the big homies who were in their 20s and known for their gang and alleged criminal involvement. The younger teenage boys of the crew got caught up in the sweep by default. Being Black, poor, and from this neighborhood made you guilty by association. So there they were, handcuffed and sitting on the curb, complying with the all-too-familiar drill of being stopped by the police.

The crew saw value in me from that experience and offered me the opportunity to make some real cash that could really help lessen the societal burden and pressures we were feeling. Not to mention help my mother put food on the table. At 11 years old, I would steal quarters from a jar that was under my little brother's teacher's cabinet when I would help her clean her classroom after school. The jar always seemed to replenish itself, as if someone knew our dinner that evening depended on it. From there I would go to the 99-cents store and buy three candy bars for 99 cents. I would then stand in front of the store and sell them for a dollar each, tripling my profits. I'll never forget the day my little brother turned 5 years old and I was able to take the whole family to Taco Bell to celebrate his birthday. Looking back, I wonder why my mother never questioned the mystery jar of quarters I told her I found, repeatedly. I want to believe she was just relieved that I was able to step in at a time when she legitimately couldn't. Now I had an opportunity to make real money while earning the respect and protection of my neighborhood. I was all in.

I never really liked smoking marijuana. Being high was like being trapped in a cage, and I didn't have control over when it would end. Even one puff would take me hours to come down from and if I closed my eyes, I would immediately start falling down the never-ending hole from *Alice in Wonderland*. So because I wasn't a weed head—and the guiding principle most drug dealers would try to live by was *don't get high on your own supply*—I made for a pretty good drug dealer. It was easy. The miniature ziplock bags, or sacs as we called them, would be given to me already prepared. First nickel sacs, then dime sacs, until I eventually got promoted to selling dub sacs after proving I could turn them over and bring back the revenue the same day. I basically ditched all of ninth grade, trading in an education that may help me later, for a job that would help me now. My hustle required me to be available and present at any ditch parties or random kids' houses to supply them with their high. I only showed up to school to take a test, fight whoever had the nerve to challenge either me or my siblings—fights I never started, but always finished—or because there was no money to be made that day. The money flowed easily and I was able to purchase my first pair of Jordans, fly outfits from the local fashion stores, and make sure my little sisters and brothers had all the snacks, lunch money, and goodies they needed.

I didn't realize how dangerous my job was until I accidently left my little black purse that held all of my product and cash on the Big Blue Bus. My homies who I thought loved me and had my back immediately turned on me, threatening me and my family unless I came back that night with the missing cash. They didn't give a shit that I lost it, that we were "friends," a term I learned to start unpacking and not using so loosely, or that I had been loyal, down, and took many, many risks for them. Caesar wanted his money, or else.

Fortunately, my mother had just made a bank run, taking the only cash she had to her name out of the ATM, $60, and the exact amount that I lost on the bus. I stole the money from her without thinking twice, quickly slipped out of the house and gave it to Caesar, who praised me for "making it happen," and assured me that we were good and back to normal, as if the trust and safety I thought I had, but lost, would just magically and immediately reappear. That night, my mother would learn of my drug dealing and be pissed and devastated. Our electricity would be cut off and our stomachs would be empty. But we were safe and unharmed. That's all that mattered to me at that moment. From that day forward, I would never sell drugs of any kind ever again.

Being tough, or giving the appearance of it, was easy when you have your crew, protection, and a reputation not to be fucked with. In juvenile hall, no one knew me, no one had my back. I was the new girl, a target and a new shiny punching bag waiting and bracing for the first blow. After walking in a line with our arms behind our back and forming a diamond, just like I saw the line of boys doing, we quickly made it to our dining area, which was essentially metal tables and benches that were fixed to the ground in the center of the large building that housed us. Looking around the room, there were two floors of doors lining the walls in a never-ending circle, each created specifically to cage us "super predators." That's the term criminologist John DiIulio coined when he warned and convinced the nation that the most looming threat facing our society were Black and brown children.

On the outskirts of the tables was a large, plastic rolling cart that contained our meal, already pre-packaged and ready to grab, just like at school. The only difference was that this food was way worse, and I didn't think school cafeteria food could get any worse. In line, I tried not to make eye contact with any of the other girls and kept my head lowered to hide the puffiness and redness of my eyes so that no one could tell that I had just been crying like a baby. I looked up briefly to grab my tray of food, realizing that I hadn't had anything to eat that day, outside of the bowl of Honey Nut Cheerios I had for breakfast. I was purposely saving my appetite for my one-year anniversary meal with my boyfriend at our favorite Cuban spot, Versailles on Pico and LaCienega. I was really looking forward to the large garlic prawns, white rice, black beans, and sweet plantains. Instead, my tray had a spoon of canned spaghetti, a hard bun, and a room temperature box of 2% milk. There was no cafeteria lady with a net covering her hair and a defeated, sad expression because after 50 years of surviving the harshness of this world, her life choices and inability to access the great American dream, had landed her in a school cafeteria collecting lunch tickets from poor kids that qualified for free lunch. We instead had yet another CO, towering over the cart and making sure us, terrible children, didn't take more than one tray of food that lawmakers wouldn't feed their dogs, but proudly classified our ketchup packet as a vegetable, in order to shave federal spending. At this point I was famished, and wanted nothing more than to devour the dog food we had been given. Before I did, I had to make a critical decision that could inform my very experience while in this hell. Where and with whom do I sit?

I didn't realize how calculated my decision needed to be. Naturally, I'd want to sit with the Black kids because they were my people and there is normally a comfort and safety associated with familiarity. There were only about six small tables, each big enough to fit four or five girls, so my options were slim based on available seating, or if my table of choice objected to my presence. Not surprisingly, the tables were segregated, half Black and half Mexican, or so I thought. Unlike having a Brittany, who would be excited and eager to greet and include the new girl, I was greeted with harsh eyes that spelled out very clearly that no one wanted me at their table.

"Take a seat, Chandler!" the CO behind me yelled. Apparently, my decision-making skills were holding up the line. Seeing the closest available seat was at a table with a group of who I thought were Mexican girls, but were actually El Salvadorain, I reluctantly took a seat and tried very hard to keep my head lowered, eat my meal, and make it through dinner without crying. I was not in the mental space to engage, make friends, play nice, defend myself, or even try to make sense of this place. I was processing what was happening to me, scared, uncertain of my future and what was going to happen next. I also didn't have anything against Mexican girls, I just didn't know them like that. As hard as I would try to play with them in the sandbox in elementary school, they just weren't fucking with me, so I stuck with my people. As soon as I sat down, the four girls at my table immediately started talking and laughing in Spanish. Being insecure, I assumed they were talking about me, laughing at my visible fragileness and plotting to take me down for having the audacity to sit on their turf. Glancing over at the table with the Black girls, I could see a few of them throwing sharp stares my way, probably pissed that I didn't make an effort to come sit at their table and denying them the opportunity to show me just how tough and badass they were when denying me access. It was a lose-lose situation in here, and my plan was to keep to myself as much as I could and try my best to stop fucking

crying. But, as I took the first bite of my cold spaghetti, the tears started flowing. Everything and everyone around me became a blur and I shrunk, hoping that I would become so small that I was invisible, unseen, and out of reach.

CHAPTER 4

A FTER A NIGHT of crying and surviving the deafening drip of the faucet, still of the night, and uncomfortableness of my bed, I woke to the bright, aggressive lights of the cell. It's 6 a.m. and the voice of the CO for the morning shift shouted loudly over the intercom, *"Wake up, ladies!"* Another CO walked past every cell, sharply tapping her baton on each of our doors and yelling, *"Rise and shine, ladies."* I found it odd that although the COs were all women, I didn't find the kindness and compassion I would hope to get from a mother, aunt, neighbor, church lady or someone who cared and wanted to help you do better and be better. These women were hired to bark orders, throw insults and remind us that we were little and they were big. They managed the chaos that was destined to occur when you throw a bunch of angry and lost teenagers in a room and punish them without caring to hear their side of the story. The COs were glorified babysitters with batons, pepper spray, and the power to control if you spent your day in agonizing isolation, or amongst your peers engaging in everything but rehabilitation.

I quickly undressed out of the pajamas I was given, which reminded me of the big gown you're handed at the hospital, and put back on my uniform of shame. We had only minutes to dress and step outside of our door, many of us still yawning and rubbing our eyes, and others pouting for having to get up so early. We walked past the showers, where I cringed, and back to the dining hall for breakfast. The night before, after managing to slop down my meal through the tears and snot from my crying episode, we were marched off for showers before bed. The showers reminded me of the ones at the Santa Monica Pier that you use to rinse off all the sand after a day of running from waves, building sandcastles, and having one of your siblings or friends bury you in the sand, leaving only your small head erected and giving the appearance that you're standing up. The only difference is that these showers had a thin plastic curtain that covered about 75% of the shower in length and width, and a soap dispenser with bright, pink, slime-like soap that we used to wash both our hair and body. There were three showers. We formed three lines, wrapped in the short, stiff towels we were given that almost fully exposed the curvy and overweight girls and gave brief privacy to the others. While showering, we were given strict orders to take one minute to rise, one minute to wash, and one additional minute to rinse again, for a total of three minutes to shower. Aside from the thin, scant shower curtain, we had no privacy. The other girls were almost forced to look in our direction while we showered, because what else would they possibly do while waiting in line for their turn?

While we waited and watched, or tried not to watch, we quickly learned who was on their period, or who was struggling with a yeast infection, based on us watching the blood or thick white substance mix with the bright pink liquid they called soap, splashing onto the dingy, white tiled floor and sliding down the drain. When it was my turn, I tried my best to slide the curtain as close to the front of the shower and stand still in the middle, so as not to expose the parts of me that already had too many eyes on them that day. My hair was still a mess and I tried my best to rinse it out so that it was at least soft enough to grind the thin, plastic comb we were given through it, and put in a few braids—since we were not allowed hair ties—so that I could at least make it through the next day with some sense of dignity. The soap made my hair feel like a Barbie doll's hair and definitely was not Black-girl friendly. By the time I managed to rinse it out, my hair was a matted mess and my time was up. I prayed the water and soap that dripped from my hair at least made its way down to the parts I wasn't afforded enough time to wash. That night, I spent hours working the small comb through my now matted, plastic-feeling hair and managed to create two of the most hideous French braids that I tied at the end with rolled toilet paper, so that they wouldn't unravel.

Now at breakfast, I kept to myself and ate the thawed breakfast burrito that was small enough to fit in the palm of my hand. *"What are you in here for?"* the short Black girl with cornrows across from me asked. *"I...I,"* I start to stutter, now asking myself and trying to remember what the hell I'm in here for. *"Petty theft,"* I replied, wondering if I should have said something more impressive, like robbery or grand theft auto. *"Yeah, a lot of us are here for stealing shit. What you steal?"* Caught off guard by her response, I was embarrassed to admit that I got caught stealing a pack of underwear for my little sister and an orange T-shirt for myself. Clearly, if petty theft was a common reason for locking kids up, my ignorance of the matter and risk-taking for such immaterial items in the grand scheme of things would definitely put me at the bottom of the totem pole here. *"You know, fresh gear from the mall,"* I lied. Before she could respond, the CO starts calling out names, *"Anderson, Chandler, Martinez, Smith, line it up, you have court."*

Court? I thought to myself. I guess I hadn't realized that I would have an opportunity to speak to a judge and defend myself, tell them this was all a mistake, and that I'm sorry and will never, ever, steal again. I got excited and quickly jumped up, saying nothing to the girl who was sitting across from me. No *"Talk to you later,"* or *"Have a great day."* I was planning on never seeing any of them, ever again. My days of watching *Judge Judy* with my mom were about to pay off. I knew not to say anything crazy and to own my shit, and that's what I was prepared to do. I would tell the judge that I was normally a straight-A student, loved to read and explore nature and was really a kind, giving, and compassionate person. I would tell her that life unfortunately sucked at the moment, that we were poor and that I did what I felt was necessary to help take care of my siblings and myself, and minimize or eliminate them from experiencing any of the social pressures I was forced to absorb for all of us. I was always a pretty articulate girl, could pronounce my words just like the white folks and even use big, fancy ones when I really wanted to show off a new word I experienced in a novel I read. *"Oh, wait till she sees that I'm not one of these other kids that probably did something worthy of them being locked in this concrete institution for misfits,"* I thought.

As we quickly formed a line and prepared to walk with our arms behind our backs and hands forming a diamond, we were approached by another CO in charge of transporting us to the adjoined court building less than a five-minute walk away. She pulls out four pairs of handcuffs and one by one, tells us to stretch out our arms and begins to shackle our wrists. She then begins to shackle our ankles and connects a chain from the wrist shackles to the ankle shackles, giving us just enough leg span to walk a foot at a time. In complete shock and feeling the most degraded I had ever felt in my life, I began to reflect on a movie my parents had us watch called *Roots*, where Kunta Kinte was captured in Africa and sold into American slavery. He wore similar shackles, only mine lacked the rust and neck collar that came with his. I recall thinking how awful and sad that movie was, but was completely disassociated from the reality that modern-day slavery was still occurring in the form of mass incarceration. What happened in *Roots* was so far removed from anything that I would ever experience, or so I thought, but standing there shackled and with other kids preparing to walk the plank to the courtroom that held our fate, started to feel uncomfortably familiar.

Sitting on a bench shackled and staring at blank white walls in a hallway that led to the back entrance of the courtroom where inmates enter, we were joined by other kids who had been bussed in from other camps or detention centers for their court hearings. I was approached by a frail, tired-looking white man who stood about 5'9", had shaggy hair and glasses that came straight out of the 90s. In his arms, he tightly gripped an accordion file case that held the records of the accused, arrest reports, case reports, and Lord knows what else.

He called out, *"Chandler, Charity Chandler?"*

I looked up and responded, *"Yes."*

"Hello, I'm your Public Defender, Mr. Roberts, and will be representing you today."

Having no idea what Public Defender meant, I assumed he meant lawyer and said *"Ok."*

"You were charged with petty theft," he stated. *"When we go into the courtroom, I will speak for you. Only speak if the judge asks you a question directly. They go in alphabetical order, so you'll be one of the first ones called. I'll see you there in a few."*

He offered me a slight smile, looking exhausted from a night of probably reading all the files in his arms that he must have only received hours before, or early that morning. He proceeded to get up while looking at the same piece of paper he called my name from earlier.

"Sir, wait, can I tell you what happened? Are we going to plan my defense?" I asked. I imagined that having an attorney meant that I had someone that would advocate for me, hear my side of the story, understand the context behind why I did what I did, and be prepared to advocate for solutions that could help my family and prevent me from making such a stupid mistake in the future. I needed him to know that I was a good kid who made poor decisions, like most kids do, and that I didn't deserve to spend another day in this jail.

"It's ok. I do this everyday. I'll handle it. I have your file and all the information right here," he said while sadly patting his accordion file. I caught a quick glance at his list, and there were at least seven other names, all of whom I assumed

he needed to also quickly identify and speak with before court started in 30 minutes.

I took a deep breath and told myself to trust the system. *"There is no way they will keep me in here, and I'll still have a chance to speak with the judge. She'll understand,"* I thought. Sitting back, and looking down at my hands that are bearing the weight of the iron shackles I was wearing, I began to wonder what the judge would think of me and how it would affect my outcome. When we were little, my parents would try their best to make sure we looked nice and presentable when going before important people or during important events, like church, funerals, weddings, or the welfare building. We were poor, but presentation and how others perceived us seemed important to them. I never really understood why until that moment when it hit me like a punch to the stomach. Looking around, we all looked like a hot-ass mess. The Black girls all had frizzy, messy hair that was either tied together with rolled toilet paper or braided as well as one could braid with the thin mini comb we were given. Those combs may have worked fine for the Hispanics and the lone white girl, but it definitely did no justice for our hair. The boys were lucky, at least most of them, because they didn't have much hair to deal with. The ones who did looked just as bad as us girls, with matted afros or unkempt braids, the perfect image of your stereotypical super predator.

I didn't look like myself at all. I normally rocked a slick bun to the back, with a side part and tons of PRO STYL gel that would keep it in place all day, or a bun that was aggressively brushed up and sat on the very top of my head, with my baby hairs purposely forming mini waves across my crown. Here my lips were dry and cracked, and as I parted them to allow my tongue to peek out to quickly provide a layer of hydration from my saliva, I could taste the blood that had dried from one of the cracks that had formed. We didn't have mirrors in our bathrooms or cells, so I had no idea I looked as bad as I did. We also weren't given lotion for our body or face, so our skin was dry and ashy, with the ash more visible on the Black or darker-skinned kids. We looked like a bunch of rough kids who no one would want to engage, let alone show sympathy and support for in a courtroom. We looked bad, delinquent, troubled, and even criminal according to how those in power so intentionally and thoughtfully created the stereotype and image of what a super predator would look like. The only thing missing when I thought of a super predator was foam spouting from our mouths and really long, dirty, fingernails. Fuck. Now headed into the courtroom to plead my case, I was consumed with how I looked and how I would convince the judge that I not only wasn't the person described in her file, but I also wasn't the person she was looking at.

Dept. 109 were the numbers on the door I entered, shackled, disheveled, and giving the appearance of guilt and condemnation. In the room were the judge, a lady behind a typewriter, a sheriff, and a panel of three people facing the judge—one of which was the public defender guy, Mr. Roberts, who I spoke with earlier. Directly behind them were a few benches where worried family members and friends of the incarcerated youth who were being heard, sat to observe and see their loved one who went missing via what I would describe as kidnapping for societal improprieties that didn't always justify imprisonment.

My mother wasn't among them. I figured she wouldn't sacrifice a day of work and pay to be there for me. This also wasn't her first rendezvous. She'd experienced many courtrooms and days off with my older sister and knew something I didn't know just yet, but was about to find out. The guard walked me in and motioned for me to sit next to my attorney, which I did. The judge, attorneys, and lady behind the typewriter did not bother to look up at me. From what I could tell, they were trying to quickly scan the file and documents that sat before them to get caught up on my case. Even my attorney, who offered me a quick short glance as the chair next to him was pulled out by the guard, and not because of chivalry, but because my hands were subdued, went right back to reading and trying to remember who the hell the girl was that he spoke to no more than 30 minutes ago.

Without my testimony, it was clear that my fate rested on the words coming from those papers, the interpretation of its readers, any bias and racism that may be crouching below and ready to strike like a cougar patiently waiting for its prey, and the desires of all parties to truly invest in supporting a young Black girl who was marked from the beginning. As I sat down and looked up at the judge, I was amazed by how much she actually looked like Judge Judy. She was white, with a short haircut that rested right below her chin. By the way her black robe swallowed her frame and her chest barely rising high enough to fit the bench, you could tell she was small and petite and that the court probably needed to invest in better chairs. Her face bore the lines of many frowns and furrowed eyebrows. Her eyes, sharp, frozen, and unreadable. Looking up, she called the court to order and began stating what I had been accused of, not telling me, or asking me. Stating, as a fact. My lawyer softly reminded me to not speak unless asked a question directly. I sighed.

The judge proceeded to ask if we admit or deny the violation of petty theft. Mr. Roberts admitted on my behalf and requested that my punishment be light since I was a first-time offender. I wanted so badly to interject and say something. *"Why aren't they asking me anything directly? Why am I not given the opportunity to admit, or deny, or provide reasoning behind why I did what I did? Light punishment? Was my night in hell not punishment enough?"* I immediately started to feel confused, intimidated, overwhelmed, and emotional. My head started to get cloudy and dizzy as I heard the judge spew out legal terminology and jargon that I didn't understand. Then I heard, *"Minor Chandler will be detained as a delinquent ward of the court for 180 days at Eastlake Juvenile Hall. Court hearing is scheduled for January 13th, 2003, 8:30 a.m."*

My body froze and I tried to shout *"No!"* but my throat closed and I felt as if I was literally and painfully choking on every word that I tried to say. Mr. Roberts could tell that I was worked up and very calmly said, *"We'll speak right after this."* Although my body was frozen, stiff and numb, I could feel the tears rushing down my face, blurring my vision and adding a brief moment of salty hydration to my dry, cracked lips. I felt the guard tap my left shoulder and begin to lift my elbow, letting me know that it was time to go and for the next kid to take my place. I could hear the family and friends of other kids behind me sniffling, sad and shifting uncomfortably on the hard wooden benches.

They were not sad for me, but for what the prospects of my sentencing meant for their loved ones who may have committed similar, or worse acts.

In less than five minutes, I became a permanent number on a roster of delinquents. In less than five minutes, my world shattered. In less than five minutes, I was told in more ways than one that I did not matter; that my story, my truth, my life experiences were meaningless and the context behind why I did what I did held no weight next to the piece of paper that summarized who I was and what my worth was in this world. The six strangers who witnessed and participated in it all—the judge, the bailiff, my public defender, county counsel, the district attorney, and the court reporter—all sat unbothered and unscathed by this incredible injustice. In less than five minutes, it was spelled out with brutal clarity that I could not trust the people who I thought were in positions to protect, serve, offer support, and help me to actually do it. I was the threat and the person who the world needed protection from. What I did was worthy of criminalization and punishment. One hundred and eighty days of punishment, to be exact.

CHAPTER 5

I T ALL MADE sense now why there was so much chaos in the halls. No one gave a damn about us. We were not sentenced and sent to a place that cared about our well-being or helping us get on a path toward the straight and narrow. How could they do anything on our behalf without affording us the one thing that mattered the most: our story, our voice and our agency? There was no mention of any services I would receive while detained, no mentoring recommended or that letter 'R' they had written on everything for rehabilitation. Or, maybe it didn't need to be verbally stated in court but just happened as a part of my confinement. I would see. I was allowed a phone call to my mother not too long after being told that I wouldn't be able to protect my four younger sisters and brothers from the realities of our neighborhood that I tried my hardest to shield them from. I got anxious wondering what they would do without me. Who was going to walk them to school and pick them up everyday? Who was going to heat up the bean and cheese burritos, or make sure they didn't burn themselves with the cup of noodles? Who was going to make sure no one fucked with them? That was my job, and now I wouldn't be able to do any of it. This sentence was for me, but affected my whole family. *"God, I hope Harmony doesn't do anything crazy while I'm in here,"* I thought to myself while the chrome, cold payphone rang and rang. My mom finally answered and I immediately started crying, begging her to come rescue me, visit me, anything.

"Mom," I whimpered, like a child begging to be taken off punishment, *"I am so sorry. I'll never steal again, I promise,"* I cried. *"Mom, you know I'm a good kid. You know I try my best to help our family. You know I'm always there for you when you need me. You can't let them do this to me."*

"Charity, you made your bed, now you have to lay in it. I can't visit you, I can't risk losing my job. You chose this path and these are the consequences," she stated.

"Chose?!" I shouted. *"I didn't choose this. I didn't choose to be poor. I didn't choose to be in this family. I didn't choose to live in that awful neighborhood. You chose that for us!"* I screamed angrily, now foaming at the mouth like a real super predator. How could she say that? How could she dare think that I wanted any of this mess? I didn't wake up one day wanting to sell drugs, or be in a gang, or have to succumb to stuffing a $4 pack of underwear and $8 T-shirt in my pants. No one wakes up wanting to do any of that. If the choice were mine, I would be on an island reading *The Babysitters Club*, Judy Blume, or my favorite American Girl books. If the choice were mine, I would be swimming, laughing, playing, and enjoying my favorite fruits while relaxing under the sun— like the cherries, mangoes and pomegranates that we could never afford, but got to taste on occasion. Why the hell couldn't adults who knew everything understand that? We don't have the luxury of choosing our lives. Our lives

choose us, and if the adults aren't able to protect us from it, we either survive it, or we don't.

Hanging up the phone, I was left even more devastated and defeated than I was when walking out of the courtroom. I never felt so alone and scared in my life. I wondered if my dad knew I was in here. We hadn't spoken much since the night I was raped by my green-eyed boyfriend and my mother kicked me out of the house at 14 years old for losing my virginity. She didn't notice the pain in my voice or sorrow on my face as I tried to stand there convincing myself that I was strong and I was ok. All that mattered was that I had sex. No questions were asked, no motherly talk about my health, diseases, or pregnancies. I was tainted and dirty in her Christian eyes, and was told I couldn't even sit my nasty behind on my cheap bed in the section 8 room I shared with my two other sisters. I called my dad crying and he immediately told me how to get to him, having no car himself to pick me up.

I took the bus from West LA to Compton, riding down Alondra Blvd and looking at all of the houses, apartments, and schools I recognized from when we used to have our visits with our dad after my parents divorced and before the judge stripped my father of pretty much all of his rights, while ordering him to pay so much child support that he wasn't sure how he was going to survive himself. The only difference this time was that the bus didn't take me to the old house he proudly rented that had our names carved in the fresh cement, when it was poured. The bus took me to a self-storage center not too far from Enterprise Middle School. My dad was waiting out front and embraced me with the warmest and kindest hug. He also didn't ask me any questions about what happened, but he wasn't mad at me either, so I took the win. I was confused why we were there, and figured he had some of my old belongings in the storage and we were going to grab them before heading to his place. The summer between 8th grade and high school just started and I was kinda excited at the idea of having my dad all to myself for a while. While walking to the unit we eventually stopped at, I noticed it was a bit cracked open with an orange electrical cord running from inside the unit, to an outlet about 20 feet away. Lifting the clanky sheet metal door, it exposed a well-lit 10' x 15' unit that had around 12 boxes stacked neatly in the back, my dad's tall living room lamp that had four lights arching from the base and reminded me of a four-headed dragon, dad's living room couch, and a mattress laying on the floor with a blanket on top and one of his favorite *Lord of the Rings* novels. Next to the mattress was a gallon-size water bottle that was a quarter of the way filled with a yellow liquid that I later found out was urine.

Was dad living here? Would I be living here? That summer, I did indeed experience living in a storage unit and having to choose between suffocating under my sheet because the storage was so hot, or getting bit up by mosquitos the size of a golf ball. Some days I would wake up with my face completely covered in mosquito bites to the point that it looked like I got in a really bad fight and got my ass beat. After much complaining, my dad traded living in the storage he was renting to squatting in an abandoned property on Crenshaw and 63rd, in exchange for helping a friend attempt to get his old Datsun back up and running. The lone house sat on a bare lot with about six vehicles that were probably better off going to the junkyard. Similar to the storage, we had a mattress on the floor, no running water, and an unflushable toilet that smelled of the urine and feces its last occupant left. We still utilized peeing in the water bottle if we couldn't hold it overnight and frequenting fast-food restaurants and libraries when we needed to use the bathroom during the day.

For some reason, that summer was unbearably hot. When my father finally realized having me was too much, but being too proud to let my mother know that, he reached out to my long-lost godfather to see if I could stay with him and his wife until he got back on his feet. My godfather Earl's house was nice and in the Park Mesa Heights neighborhood of Los Angeles, not too far from where we were squatting. I had three meals a day, a computer to play solitaire on, a working toilet, and an air-conditioned room. His wife was very nice, but quiet and timid. Everything was going fine until he decided it would be appropriate to start grooming me to be his second wife. He didn't touch me or do anything weird, thank God, but seriously posed the question to my father who punched him in the face, told me to grab my things, and we were off to my mother, who reluctantly took me back. If my dad knew I was in jail, surely he would try to save me and get me out. But I had no number for him. I just prayed that somehow he found out.

While being escorted back to the complex we were being housed in, I started to feel incredibly embarrassed and ashamed. I thought for a fact that I wouldn't see any of these girls again and knowing that the Charity I presented earlier was weak—crying all over the place and keeping her head down—made me worry about how my 180-day stint here would play out. I didn't want to be an easy target. I wanted to be left alone. I wanted to continue crying and praying that this was all a scary dream I would soon be waking up from. When we returned from court, I wasn't escorted to my room where I could cry and scream into my pillow in private, but to another building where all the kids were in classrooms, summer school I supposed. I was taken first to a room where I was told I needed to take an assessment to see what grade level I was at. How could I possibly take a test right now? I was trying my best not to lose it. My soul was grieving the fact that I would be in jail for 180 days. I was scared. I didn't know any of these strangers. I didn't trust them. I needed a hug. Some vaseline for my lips. A sip of water. A nap. Not a test.

After taking the annoying assessment that I clicked through without any thought, clarity, or certainty, I was taken to a classroom with about 10 other girls of all different ages and grades. We were all given a worksheet that was similar to the ones I was given in third grade. I guessed I'd be learning how to "carry the one" all over again. While in the classroom, the girls were doing everything but their worksheet. I tried my best to stick to myself and focus on the worksheet to keep from crying. I noticed a mini shelf nearby with chapter books and prayed that we would be allowed to read them. I didn't have the strength or courage to ask for one. I couldn't risk being told no and taking another loss that day. That would have broken me completely. But I could have used another world to escape to, another character to embody and an exciting adventure to embark on, even if only for a moment.

While in class, I stared down at my paper, sobbing and watching my tears fall on the worksheet. I could hear the other girls laughing, roasting each other, shit-talking, and making various origamis, or small rolled paper pellets out of their worksheets that they would flick at each other. We weren't being taught. There was no instruction for our work and the two COs were taking turns watching us and having their own conversation. One of the girls, Johnson, invited me to join her table. While hesitant, I went over, not necessarily because I wanted a friend or to find my posse, but because she was big as hell and I wasn't going to risk getting on anyone's bad side. Johnson, like me, was also 16 years old, about 6' tall, and definitely weighed over 200 pounds. She was as dark as the night and had the tiniest little ponytail sitting on top of her head. Definitely someone we would have roasted for being a chicken head. She had really deep dimples and very high cheekbones. She was beautiful, but a different kind of beautiful from what we were conditioned to believe.

"*Whatchu in here foe?*" she asked. This time I wasn't going to give the same weak response I gave earlier, so I mustered the strength to say, "*You know, stealing shit, got caught because of this dumb-ass bitch.*"

"*Damn, that's fucked up. They always trying to lock us up for some dumb shit.*"

"*Yea, tell me about it,*" I said.

I figured it was time for me to ask her what she was locked up for, and although I really didn't want to know, I asked anyway.

"*Prostitution,*" she said. "*They caught me with a trick, let that nigga drive off and they took me in. This my third time in this bitch.*"

In complete shock, I say, *"What? What's prostitution?"*

She started laughing along with some of the other girls. Apparently, I was the only one who was completely oblivious to what prostitution was. What I learned was that teenaged girls were essentially being put in jail for being raped by grown men, because children couldn't consent to sex, and they were allowed to drive off and remain free. I was shocked and furious all at the same time. The other girls at the table were all in jail for the same thing, that's why they hung out with each other. They had a familiar background they didn't seem ashamed of, or bothered by. There was a sense of pride and naivety as they spoke about their pimps and all that they did for them. They glamorized how much money they made, but didn't get to keep. They cracked jokes about how their pimps would beat their ass, punch them in the face, or burn them with cigarettes if they didn't bring home enough money, looked another man in the eyes, or failed to call them "daddy." Daddy was always there waiting for them when they got out. He always took them to get a fresh set of nails, a new wig and an outfit from Rainbow, or their favorite hood fashion boutique.

These girls were so broken and delusional that they were willing to do anything their pimps asked of them to maintain a fake sense of protection, love, and family. They were brainwashed, threatened, beaten, and kidnapped into this lifestyle. Clearly no girl, no child, wakes up and independently thinks, *"Let me sell my body to strange grown men in exchange for money that I can't keep and quotas, that if I don't make, will get me a black eye and busted lip."* So why were they in here? Why weren't they being rescued by these lawyers, judges, and COs? Why were they being punished for something I couldn't begin to imagine being a crime on their part. What in the entire hell was going on? I had so many questions, but just sat and tried my best to process all of their horror stories—near death encounters on the "hoe stroll," and what they were planning on continuing doing once they got out—without looking too shocked and mortified.

I noticed during our little talk that one of the girls, Morgan, was crushing something up that looked like a pill and another girl, Chappell, was sharpening the end of a metal paper clip she managed to get ahold of, probably from the stack of worksheets.

"You ready, bitch?" Morgan, a skinny, short, caramel-complected girl of 15 years asked Stevens, also 15 years old with bright red hair that you could tell she dyed recently by the red stains around the crown of her head.

"Yeah, bishh, let's do this!"

Stevens, using the paper airplane she made out of the math worksheet, takes half of the crushed powder Morgans had and spreads it into a neat thin line. She then lowers her head, presses down on her left nostril, and snorts it right up her nose. Wide-eyed like a deer in headlights, I'm completely caught off guard by this new way of kids taking drugs. I was only used to weed and would hear of a drug called sherm from time to time, but never knew about snorting prescription medications. What came next was even more shocking and disturbing. Morgan took the sharpened paper clip from Chappelle. Stevens stuck out her tongue, and Morgan quickly and fiercely stabbed the middle of her tongue, took out the sharp paperclip and replaced it with one of the teeth from our small plastic combs. Just as quickly as I witnessed my first tongue piercing, I witnessed the whole left side of Stevens' face turn gray and she started to frantically wail her arms while trying to scream, but only a deep-choked coughing sound came from her throat. The COs, now realizing that something was up at the corner table, annoyingly rushed over to break up what they thought was a fight, and told everyone to stand against the wall. Seeing that Stevens was in need of medical attention, she was taken to the infirmary and we were all rushed back to our rooms.

We later found out that Morgan struck a nerve and Stevens' left side of her face was completely paralyzed. Stevens, now unable to really talk, told the COs she tried to pierce her own tongue. Snitching was against the hood code and apparently juve code as well. After Stevens left the infirmary, she was put in solitary confinement for two weeks as her punishment. The next time we saw her she not only looked crazy, she was crazy. The pain from her injuries coupled with the mental and emotional agonizing reality of what that one mistake would cost her, plus the social isolation and lack of support after such a traumatizing experience did a number on her mental health. I vowed that day to never, ever, get my tongue pierced.

CHAPTER 6

MY 180 DAYS inside was a complete reality shock. Despite the poverty I experienced, the little hood antics I engaged in, stealing from stores and selling weed to help put food in our stomachs and clothes on our back, it was nothing compared to the realities many of the girls I encountered lived and experienced daily. The girls I came across ranged from 12 to17 years old and were being locked up, punished, and criminalized because they lived in a world that wouldn't allow them to be children and forced them to grow up faster than they should have. They were subjected to a world that didn't see them as children if their skin was too dark, accent too thick, or if they came from an over surveilled and policed neighborhood. They had to tolerate a world that adultified and sexualized Black girls and failed to see us as needing protection and saving. This hell was filled with mainly Black and brown kids. I figured they probably kept the white kids in a different jail, maybe one with better food, softer beds, and where they weren't being called lunatics and dumb asses by the COs. Clearly the lone white girl I went to court with was here by accident, and I haven't seen her since court, so they probably figured it out and put her in the jail for white people. Or, maybe there wasn't a jail for white people. I had so many questions.

It was very clear that we were being punished and warehoused in this mental complex of shame because our oppression on the outs wasn't enough. The number of occupied beds kept growing because those in power found it more profitable to predict and invest in our downfall, than invest in preventing our outcomes. The education we received was laughable and held us even further back from being on grade level, or being able to catch up when we returned home. There was no counseling or mentoring, only mass on Sundays that most of us signed up for just to get out of our rooms at the expense of being told that we needed salvation from our sins. What we really needed was protection from the adults in there who took their adult aggressions out on children that lacked power. The insults we received, misdirected anger, pepper spraying, and threats were less about us being bad, uncontrollable kids, and more about the COs being able to punish someone for the argument they had with their significant other the night before, or stress about their rising debt, shitty job, or Lord knows what else. We were their verbal and emotional punching bags that made them feel big and powerful in a world that they too were actually small and insignificant in.

Juve taught me how to be a real gangsta, how to lie, deceive, organize for my own interest, and constantly watch my back. Juve taught me that if I went to the CO with any questions, needs, or information, that it could be used against me in a report and leveraged for my obedience. Juve taught me that the world wasn't composed of just Black, Mexican and white people, and that mistaking an

El Savadorian for a Mexican or vice versa, could get you in some real trouble. Juve taught me that little girls were getting pregnant and having babies as young as 12 years old and still being put in jail, when they should instead be getting medical and mental health attention and support. I'll never forget the day Espinoza was handcuffed and carried off to the county hospital to have her baby. She was a short 15-year-old girl, barely five feet tall, and was locked up because she got into a fight at school with another kid over cutting her in line at the cup of noodle machine. She would come back two days later crying, still handcuffed and babyless. She told us the story of being handcuffed during her delivery and considered so criminal and a flight risk that she needed to be chained down during the most painful and vulnerable time of her life.

I understood that the people on the side of incarcerating youth didn't give a fuck about us, but the nurses and doctors too? Why didn't they speak up for all the young girls whose babies they delivered in shackles? Why didn't they question this incredible injustice, this immoral and inhumane manifestation of laws and policies that treated children worse than animals? Did they believe we were criminals and dangerous? Were they afraid for their safety and grateful that little Espinoza and the girls like her would be unable to viciously attack them with their super-predator, super strength after pushing out the baby they knew would be stripped from their arms the moment they gave birth? How did these adults that were in roles and positions that gave the appearance and assumption of protection, healing and support sleep at night? Did the world know this was happening? What would they say if they did? How did Espinoza and others deal with the compounded trauma and pain of being tied down during childbirth after a life of abuse and dysfunction themselves and losing the one thing they probably wanted and needed most in this world, their baby? *"What happened to her baby?"* I wondered.

Espinoza wasn't the same after returning, and her insistence on lashing out and trying to fight anyone who had something to say about her or her baby caused me to experience something so painful, I thought I would be blinded for life. Walking to the grass area where we were able to sit outside on benches for 20 minutes and try to enjoy the sunny day and smog-filled air of Los Angeles, someone called Espinoza a "psycho babyless bitch." She immediately turned around, jumped on the other girl, grabbing her by the hair and trying to slam her head into the wall. Ignoring the calls from the COs to break it up, the two girls continued to fight, Espinoza seeing only red and suffering from the pain of losing her baby. The other girl tried to fend her off, while shocked that Espinoza was attacking her and making her best attempt to prove that she wasn't weak. The COs, without any warning, started spraying the girls with a substance from a black container that looked like a flashlight. The way they were spraying them reminded me of the time we came across a huge water bug in the house and my mother grabbing the RAID and dousing it with the deadly liquid until it stopped moving.

These girls were being sprayed like roaches and immediately started screaming, falling on the ground, covering their eyes and gasping for air. Because I was right in front of Espinoza when the altercation took place, some of the spray blew into my eyes and on my skin. Within seconds, my eyes started tearing up, burning and itching. The sting in my eyes was so bad that I couldn't see and it hurt everytime I tried to open my eyes. I could hear other girls screaming in agony, but was so consumed with my own pain that I couldn't understand why someone, anyone, wasn't rushing to save me. Screaming and crying, I could feel someone grabbing my arm, shoving me toward the other girls and shouting, *"Everyone, straight line now!"* We were then quickly marched back to our units where all but Espinoza and the girl she was fighting were forced back into our cells. I immediately pressed the small silver button on the mini sink in my cell and cupped my left hand to capture as much of the slow dispensing water as possible to rinse out my eyes. The cold water on my eyes felt like liberation from the depths of hell. After about an hour of rinsing my eyes out, I was able to lay down, catch my breath, and try to imagine away the gritty, sandy feeling under my eyelids and the new burning sensation I felt on my face and right ear where the pepper spray made contact. If I was in this much pain and discomfort, I could only imagine the torture Espinoza and the other girl must be experiencing. Those big ass COs could have easily pulled the two tiny girls apart, but instead they used their power to show us just how tough and in control they were. Juve didn't turn delinquent super predators into well-behaved children or steer us on a path of healing, transformation, and self-awareness. Juve cultivated and released children who left there worse than they went in, who were more traumatized, burning with anger, more untrusting of adults, depressed, and reliant on psychotropic medication that was used to shut us up when we were too loud, too hurt, or too emotional. Juve was filled with the strangers our parents warned us about, except these strangers were protected by even scarier strangers in the form of policies and laws, that not only empowered them, but paved the way for them to get away with the abuse, pain and mental and emotional torture we all experienced. Juve was no place for kids and changed me for the worse. I was no longer the sweet girl simply trying to survive this world, that loved to read and escape into faraway lands and adventures. I didn't know who I was anymore, but I wasn't her.

CHAPTER 7

W HEN I WAS finally released from juve, I vowed to never go back. I thought I had control over if I went back or not, and I was adamant to prove to the judge when I returned for my probation hearing in six months that I was on the straight and narrow. My mother only visited me one time while I was locked up and brought a bottle of shampoo and body wash from the dollar store that they didn't let me keep. I was still angry at her when she visited for telling the rent-a-cops to take me to jail, and I sat quietly while she preached to me and went down a list of demands she had upon my return home in a few weeks. At that point, it'd been five months since I got locked up and I knew there was nothing she could do to get me out early, so it was pointless to even ask her. I realized parents have zero control once their kids are locked up, unless they have enough money, relationships, and power, that is. While my mother barked her demands and told me how disappointed she was in me, and that she refused to let me come back home to just be a bad example to her other children, I wondered when she would shut up and ask me how I was doing. My mother was so fixated on how my decisions affected her, that she failed to situate how her decisions affected me. My mother, like all other adults I encountered, didn't have the appetite to understand why I made the decisions I made, the role they played, or the injustice they perpetuated, intentionally or unintentionally.

My mother didn't ask how I slept in this kiddie prison. If she had, I would have told her that insomnia paid me a visit every night and that on occasion I would hear one of the girls let out of her cage to hang out with the CO that was on the night shift. My mother never asked if I was eating enough. If she had, I would have told her that the food was crappy and oftentimes old and moldy, but on occasion nice white people would stop by with fresh fruit and pastries and treat us like we were poor children in need of their saving, and theirs alone. My mother never asked me how I was doing. If she had, I would have told her that I'm being strong, but that being strong is uncomfortable and awkward and even hurts at times and that I'd rather just be a kid and save being strong for later. My mother never asked if I was OK. If she had, I would have cried just from hearing those words and would have told her that I wasn't OK. I would have told her that I questioned my existence often, that I'd started to believe that I was indeed worthless like the COs said, and that I was scared of some of the girls in there. I would have told her that I'd forgotten what being OK feels like, and that I just really want to be... OK. But I didn't get any of that. When she left after our short visit was over, I knew I would never like this woman again. I hated her and us having any type of relationship seemed pointless to me. I couldn't count on her to provide my basic needs, let alone any emotional support. She was worthless to me. Completely worthless.

I guess I was lucky that she showed up to my court hearing to pick me up when it was time for me to be released. She could have left me there. The judge gave me a condition for my release in the form of six months' probation. I was told to listen to my mother, go to school, and obviously, no stealing. The only problem at this point was that I truly hated my mother. She not only told them to take me to jail, but she only visited me once to tell me how terrible I was and to manage my expectations of her while I was there. She left me all alone and scared, and I was extremely hurt by that because I always showed up for her and her kids, whether she asked for it or not. I was a true soldier for our family, ready to take on anyone who fucked with her kids, steal to feed and clothe them, and trade in my love for reading and education for our literal livelihood. Upon my release and now back at home, I followed the terms of my probation with the exception of respecting my mother and doing everything she told me if it was in opposition to addressing the real-life needs I had. I went to school, I didn't steal, but I definitely found legal ways to provide for myself. I was no longer selling nickel, dime, and dub sacks of weed, nor was I stealing food and clothing from stores. I became the school hustler who sold giant Now & Laters and Sour Belts that I would buy from Smart & Final and be up all night stuffing in snack size, off brand ziploc bags. If I was feeling real good, I'd add in Jolly Rancher wrapped Blow Pops dipped in Kool-Aid. Kids went crazy over those. I also sold batteries that I would buy really cheap at the 99-cent store and sell for three times the price to kids who were desperate to juice back up their CD player and drown out whatever their teacher was covering in geometry or biology class. To subsidize that income, I got a job at HomeTown Buffet in Gardena with my best friend, Angelina, who I lived with most of the time after I got out. It was easier to get to work from Angelina's house and catch a ride to and from school with her. Her mother was also kind to me and seemed to understand why I was making some of the decisions I was making and even condoned me living with them.

Things at home with my mom were rough. We disagreed and argued all the time. She threatened me with juve whenever she was upset, which only further fueled my anger and hatred toward her. She prohibited me from leaving the house with the exception of school, and even told me not to speak to her kids whenever we were at odds. She couldn't afford to give me lunch money and eating the school lunch was not only disgusting, but also socially unacceptable in high school. I hated working at HomeTown Buffet, but I needed bus fare to get to and from school because we no longer lived in West LA, plus clothes and food to eat. Wearing cheap clothes from the swap meet or Fallas Paredes was not an option any longer, and I was willing to trade my mother's disapproval and disappointment in me for having a job, for not getting into verbal and physical fights at school. I learned in juve the power of just beating someone's ass for looking at you the wrong way, or disrespecting you. While I didn't want to have to ever get into a fight at school over something as dumb as appearance and fashion, I was ready. I stayed ready.

Not too long before I got locked up, my mother was approved for a first-time homebuyer's program through a GAIN welfare program and we had already moved from

West LA, where I was getting into a lot of trouble, and back to South Central where I was born. The only difference this time was that we were not off of Adams and 7th Avenue. We were off of 45th and Denker between Western and Normandie, in the 40s neighborhood. We lived between Crenshaw High and Manual Arts, and my mother made the decision not to send me to my home school, Manual Arts. I think the metal detectors when we walked in not only triggered me, but reminded her of walking through the county building and being frisked and checked before continuing the humiliating and demeaning act of begging the government for money because we were still on welfare and receiving public assistance. I started the 11th grade in late January, months after the school year began. None of the work I completed in juve counted toward my high school credits, and I was so behind it was practically impossible to catch up. There were no accommodations made for me or plans to help me get back on track. No one seemed to care that I was checking in late in the school year because I was incarcerated—a point my mother made sure to make while we were in the counselor's office. Sometimes I wondered if she wanted people's sympathy for having a "delinquent" child or for people to just really think I was a horrible kid. At this point, she had already told the church and anyone who would listen, all of my business, and made me out to be some horrible kid who ran away from home, sold drugs, did drugs, stole from stores, ditched school, and cursed her mother. I mean, I did do all of those things with the exception of doing drugs, but she never understood or told them *why* I did all of those things. No one ever seemed to question or care about the *why*.

I met new male friends while hanging out or walking down the street and learned pretty quickly how easy it was to convince them to let me drive their car or even borrow it while they were at work. I was completely void of any emotion or feelings toward boys at that point and saw each of them as a means to an end. I learned in life and furthermore while in juve that the male species was not to be trusted and that we need to get what we can out of them before they take everything from us. I learned that my body—our bodies—held power and that I could use it as a means of survival. I convinced myself that I would never allow anyone to prostitute me, like the other girls in jail did, nor would I sell my body for sex. But I would be willing to use sex, or the anticipation of sex with me to get these boys and young men to do what I wanted.

I secretly wanted someone to love me and see value and worth in me, like my boyfriend Joseph did before I went to juve and ended up breaking up with him because his alcohol problem was just out of control. Imagine being too young to legally consume alcohol, yet be dependent on it. Joseph woke up and drank a 40-oz. Old English or O.E., as we would call it, for breakfast. He had a fifth of E & J for lunch, a Sisqo for snack, and whatever he could afford to get his hands on for dinner. Before going to jail, I got so drunk with him after taking a 40-oz of O.E. to the head that I was hospitalized because no one could wake me and thought I was dead. The white, gay couple whose house we got drunk at off of 3rd and Fairfax called the ambulance. No one ever questioned what these Black kids, one a minor, were doing in their home getting drunk, nor were there any consequences like there would have been if they were

Black. They were seen as the good Samaritans who saved my life, when they were really irresponsible adults who allowed me to hang out in their home with my 19-year-old boyfriend and have as much sex and drink as much liquor as our hearts desired during school hours. I thought they were very cool and nice to let us hang out in their really nice home and never thought anything of it. I also enjoyed seeing a gay relationship for the first time and learning that they were not all of the horrible things I was taught in church. In any case, I loved Joseph and he loved me, but it just didn't work out. So, I left love for the birds and no one was ever going to get my love until I was ready to give it, or at least until I met my match, which I did.

One day while sitting at the bus stop on Venice and LaBrea, ironically not too far from the police station I was previously booked at, a forest green Chevy Monte Carlo pulled up and a dark-skinned guy in light green medical scrubs leaned over, introduced himself as Monte, and asked if I needed a ride. He wasn't attractive to me and had a slightly cocked eye, but I thought he was a doctor because he had on medical scrubs and a nice car. He met my qualifications to be used as a resource for my personal gains, and I figured at the least, I could get a ride home and start plotting to use his car while he was at work. While a guy pulling over to catcall a girl may be normal to some, it was extremely offensive to me, knowing what I now knew from being locked up. I was on a mission to make any guy that thought they could take advantage of me, feel just as exploited and used as they made us feel. No one was exempt in my book. But this guy, he was different. As unattractive as I thought he was on the outside, he was unpredictably smooth and confident on the inside. He truly thought he was the most attractive thing walking and acted like it too. Although he wore medical scrubs, he was no doctor. He worked at Cedar Sinai, the hospital I was born in, cleaning up patient rooms and sanitizing medical supplies during the day, and was a gang banger and drug dealer during the night. He was from Neighborhood Rollin 60s Crip, lived in Inglewood and was two-and-a-half years older than me. After being safely dropped off at home, we exchanged Motorola chirp numbers and talked everyday for a week straight. I was fascinated and smitten by this guy. He wasn't my type, but charming. Sweet and convincing, but rough and hard. He was respected by his friends and women seemed to love him, desire him, and need him. He didn't drink or smoke, which was unusual to me. Everyone I knew was drinking or smoking, but not him. Experiencing him was different than what I would have imagined. I became extremely curious to see him in action, his life, and his world. The next week he picked me up from my mother's house and drove me to see where he lived in Inglewood. While sitting in his car on Plymouth Avenue, a few apartment buildings down from where he lived, he told me I could get in the driver's seat and drive around the block, after a whole week of convincing him that I knew how to drive and planting the seeds for him to let me borrow his car while he was at work. Excited, I put the car in drive and pressed on the gas, except I hadn't put the car into drive. I put it into reverse by accident and backed into a big trash bin that was parked in front of the curb and filled with trash. The bin then rolled back and onto a small car behind it, destroying the whole front of the car.

"Oh shit!" I said, *"Oh my God, I am so sorry!"*

"Get in the passenger seat," he said quickly as he hopped out the car and made his way around to the driver door. I hopped over the center console and sat in the passenger seat as he jumped in behind the wheel. He quickly sped off, going around the corner and parking in the Ralphs parking lot between two cars and under a tree where there was shade. He wasn't mad at me at all. Meanwhile I braced myself and expected to get yelled at, maybe slapped, something. I didn't know what to expect. But he was calm, almost unbothered and even happy. At that very moment, no more than five minutes after having his car rammed into a trash bin, he asks me to be his girlfriend. What the hell. I was completely taken off guard. I had no plans of being anyone's girlfriend and was definitely not ready or in the mood for another committed relationship. I was on a mission and had a plan to use these guys for my personal benefit, feel no remorse about it and never, ever trust any of them. But I gave in and said yes. Maybe it was the fear I had of saying no. Or, maybe it was out of guilt for crashing his car. It could have even been because deep down inside I liked this bad boy and wanted to explore not only him, but the perks and benefits that came with having an older boyfriend who had a car and made me feel safe. I said yes not knowing that this bad boy would break my heart one day, would cheat on me consistently, would verbally and physically hurt me, and would make me feel like I was his property and trapped. I said yes to the moment and to the curiosity of being a real gangsta's girl. From then on, he was my ride to work and school and like I hoped, he let me drive his car while he was at work, but not before giving me a few driving lessons and making sure I wouldn't dent

up his car again. I would go everywhere with him and he loved showing me off to his homies, friends, and relatives. I hadn't met his mom, dad, and siblings just yet, but he had a cousin who lived not too far from my mom's house off King and Western. We would hang out over there, even spend the night on her living room floor. We were always together and I started to fall for him, I started to love him. I started to need him.

Before I knew it, my six-month probation hearing was here and I was scheduled to appear in court back at Eastlake Juvenile Hall. I had work later that afternoon and knew I would be cutting it close to time depending on how long we would have to wait, so I proudly wore my Home Town Buffet uniform to court. I was excited to show the judge that I had been faithfully working, going to school, and taking care of myself. On the ride to court, I sat in my mother's car, which I hadn't done in months since first coming home and getting enrolled in school. I hated being in the car with her and surprisingly, she didn't speak to me. She completely ignored me while singing gospel music at the top of her lungs. I couldn't wait to get taken off probation and be free of them and free of her. I was now 17 years old, barely passed the 11th grade with all D's and would need to go to summer school. I had plans to never return back home. I was OK with living at Angelina's and spending the night at various locations with Monte. We had planned for him to pick me up from work that evening and drop me off at Angelina's house where we would sit parked in front of her house talking or making out.

Sitting in the hallway waiting for the bailiff to call us in was miserable, intimidating, and even frightening. I thought of the kids who were waiting in the other hallway in the back of the courtroom who were locked up and unsure of their fates. I was at least happy to be on this side where I could see the trees through the window and experience people who were dressed in normal clothes and who could walk in and out of the hallway, or even the door at their leisure. Despite the sudden awareness of the freedom that I was currently experiencing, I became anxious and uncertain of what would happen next. I quickly remembered that this place was not to be trusted and what should logically and morally happen doesn't actually happen. Not here. I assured myself that there was no way anything crazy would happen. I hadn't committed any crimes, I hadn't hurt anyone, I went to school everyday, I had a job, I was OK. I was going to be OK. I started to repeat that over and over until we were finally called in. I'm OK. I'm OK. It's going to be OK.

"Remove your belt and take your shoe strings out of your shoes," said the stern voice of the bailiff standing in front of me. Only moments before, the same judge that had imposed my first sentence and condemned me to jail for being poor and stealing underwear, read a letter out loud that was given to her from my mother. The letter said that I was running away from home everyday, doing drugs, and hanging around various boys and men all of the time. My mother wrote that I was a pimp and was always driving different men's cars. In the letter from my mother was Exhibit A, the cream-colored plastic cap from a Black & Mild that I accidently left on my window sill that was her evidence that I was on drugs. Hearing about me driving young men's cars was her proof that I was a pimp and my

disrespect toward her, as exclaimed in shrewd detail in her letter, was causing my younger siblings to rebel. She felt she was losing control of her home. The judge, looking disappointed and sad for my mother and upset with me, boldly stated that I was in violation of my probation, that I was incorrigible, and deemed a runaway every time I left the house to go to work, or stay at Angelina's. As punishment, she ordered me back to jail. In that unconceivable moment, my heart dropped and hit the floor. It fell so fast and so hard that it metaphorically shattered into a thousand tiny pieces. I was certain it was beyond repair. The judge didn't ask me about my work uniform, or how school was going. She didn't ask me how I was doing, if I needed anything, or what I thought about the letter. She didn't ask for my side of the story, to defend myself or clear up any of the crazy claims like me being a pimp, which was insane. I had no voice, no power, and no control. I was once again told by this court that I was worthless and my life held zero value. What only mattered was how people experienced me, not my actual life. How could she just put me back in jail? How could she deem me unworthy of change without even asking me any questions directly? How could she just believe my mother? How could my mother write those things? *Why* would my mother write those things? Why would she go out of her way to write a letter to the court? I've never seen my mother write a letter in her life. Was I that bad? Was I wrong for feeling so hurt and abandoned by her that my only solace and refuge was to stay as far away as possible? The only times I was disrespectful or rude were when she tried to force her God on me, her gospel music on me, and her lectures about my unholiness on me. I wanted nothing to do with her, or her God. I was broken. She broke me. They broke me, and I'm the one being punished? I'm the bad guy? Fuck this bitch. Fuck both of these bitches.

CHAPTER 8

I SPENT THE NEXT four months—120 days, 2,880 hours, 172,800 minutes, ten million, three hundred and sixty-eight seconds—of my life back in the hell hole I vowed to never go back to. I was certain I would never end up back there, but apparently not liking your mother was a crime and worth wasting taxpayer dollars for. Walking into juve was different this time. I wasn't the weak little fake gangsta that went in the first time. I didn't cry. I wasn't afraid. I walked in with my head held high, shoulders back, and with an anger burning so bright and so deep that I wished a bitch would step to me. I wished someone would say something, anything, out of pocket to me. I needed an excuse to punch someone in their fucking face. I wanted to. No one tried me though. Bummer. This time I was only in a cell for a week and was moved to the halls dormitory style housing called Alpha and Omega where the "good" kids were housed, which was weird because I thought we were all here because we were bad. I guess my offense wasn't too scary after all, and because the staff at this point knew me and knew I wasn't a threat, I was gifted with a bunk bed and open-space living with about 20 other girls.

Because of the new unit I was in, I only had to interact with the same girls, which changed on occasion as old girls were released and new ones were confined. My unit consisted of the "good girls" so we didn't have to worry about any fighting, drug use, or pepper spraying. The COs were also friendlier, but still very much needing to show and prove that they were big and we were little. There were petty disagreements here and there, but the girls were on their best behavior most of the time, fearing that one day they may have to revisit a cell if they weren't. I was never a social butterfly. I always stuck to a strong friend or two who was like-minded and not into drama, which actually meant that I never really had many friends at all. I hated small talk about boys, makeup, and fashion. I despised conversations where you're gossiping or talking shit about someone, which ironically was how most friendships were formed on the outs and in here. Because of the dormitory style of sleeping and living, all we could do was talk or read, and sometimes I wished I was back in the cell and away from all the noise.

What fascinated me about the "good girls" here was that we all shared similar backgrounds. We all experienced roaches, sharing a room with multiple people, hand-me-down clothes, food stamps and hunger, and could name the same foods or snacks we ate. Like the frozen Jose Ole Chimichangas that you normally just popped in the microwave, but learned to fry in a pan, add a slice of government cheese, and dip in ketchup to try to convince yourself that you're not eating a 25-cent burrito for the fourth time in a week. Or the staple of most poor people's homes, a 10-cent cup of noodle or Top Ramen. The debates over which was better were hilarious. I was team Top Ramen for taste, but definitely the cup of noodle for convenience and not having to wash dishes after. Us Black girls bonded with the Hispanic girls over our shared love for elotes, shaved ice, and fruit cups covered in lime, salt, chamoy, and tajin. I made a point to proudly state that my best friend, Angelina, was half Mexican and half Jamaican and that her families on both sides had immigrated to America, some documented and many undocumented. When I lived with her I got to experience her mother's Mexican side of the culture, although Angelina tried very hard to separate herself from it. She wanted to be Black, refused to learn or speak Spanish, and absolutely cursed her flat butt. I personally loved that her family could speak Spanish and still had ties to Mexico. I never understood what her problem was, but I was happy nonetheless to use my friendship with her as leverage to feel relatable with the Hispanic girls here.

Many of us experienced some form of trauma. Alcoholic and drug-addicted parents was a common theme as many of their parents used drugs to numb the pain of their own trauma and suffering through poverty, joblessness, a loss of a partner to jail or death, and feeling defeated. Many of us were being raised by single mothers, had an incarcerated parent, been raped, hit by an adult out of anger, or told in one way or another that there was regret for our being born. Many of us were forced to raise and protect our younger siblings and took beatings for them, laid down on our backs in place of them, and gave up our share of food for them. Many of the girls fell for older guys who convinced them they loved them, but only used them as pawns to drive getaway cars, take the blame for their crime, or sell themselves for sex to show them just how much they loved them back. These girls never really had an opportunity to just be kids, to make mistakes and be guided in the right direction, to get it wrong and be helped along the way. They were expected to know everything and be everything without any knowledge or teaching along the way. If they got it wrong, which they did often, they were punished, and always harshly. They were never good enough for the people who claimed to love them. They were only seen for their value and the utility for the person or the people who were doing the taking. These girls were good. They were kind, they were valuable, they were worthy, they were beautiful. But no one ever told them these things. No one ever told us these things. So we accepted the filthy words that were thrown at us. We embraced and internalized the anger, the hatred, pain, failures, and inadequacies that others projected onto us. We stopped caring and living. We just existed.

My four months went by pretty quickly. When your body is numb and you no longer care about anything, everyday feels the same, the patterns are repeated, the routines are like clockwork. You wake up, eat breakfast, go to fake school, eat lunch, do nothing, an activity here or there, more of nothing or talking, maybe a new book, dinner, shower, bed. Then repeat. We didn't celebrate birthdays or holidays, unless it was Thanksgiving or Christmas and the charitable, well-intended white people came with their baskets of cheap gifts and journals for us to write in. But we could never keep any of it because contraband was prohibited and we could only enjoy it for the moment.

During Thanksgiving, we'd get a burrito that was delicious compared to the rest of the food we normally ate, and reminded us of the chimichanga burrito that we were tired of but missed and wished we had. The holidays inside weren't too hard for most of us because we never really got shit anyway and were used to being disappointed, so being locked away was just another day. Some of the girls took being inside during the holidays pretty hard though and would talk about the meals their families were probably cooking, the holiday traditions they enjoyed, the gifts their parents told them they would be getting and would be waiting for them when they got out. I was jealous of the kids who had something or someone to look forward to. I had Monte and was excited about that. I did look forward to seeing him, and the COs would let me call him on occasion. I often wondered what he was doing while I was locked up. I never thought he would be cheating on me, or anything like that. He convinced me that I was the one and only one, and I believed him. I at least had peace of mind while locked up and would be so sorry for the other girls and their stories of being cheated on. I was ready to get out of there. I didn't have a plan for when I did. I was tired of starting over. I was 17 years old at that point and couldn't wait to be 18 and on my own, away from my mother, her rules and her shit.

I got my wish earlier than I had expected on the day I was to be released, the Monday of Christmas week. My mother never appeared for my hearing and no one was there to pick me up this time. I was completely abandoned with nowhere to go. I figured that maybe she just couldn't call off work and would pick me up later. I asked if someone else could pick me up and take me home, thinking of my boyfriend Monte. They clearly knew something that I didn't, and it was that my mother did not want me to come back home. One by one she was getting rid of the children she never wanted and using the convenience of the system to do it. She got rid of my older sister at 12 years old, I was next at 16 years old, and my sister right under me had already also gone to juvenile hall but a different one called Los Padrinos in Downey. During my court hearing, where I was to be released to the custody of my mother after serving my time, the same judge handed me over to the Department of Children and Family Services (DCFS) instead, and I became what they called a foster kid.

I was anxious all over again at the thought of going to another foreign place. I didn't want to go home but I was willing to suck it up and suffer through it until I turned 18 in May, as opposed to living with another family. I recall visiting my older sister at her foster home off of 81st and Crenshaw. After spending years between juvenile halls, lock-down placements, and group homes all because, she too, was found to be disrespectful and incorrigible toward my mother, my older sister finally made it to a regular home with a foster mom and new foster siblings. I always hated that I was robbed of being able to grow up with my big sister. I resented her for leaving me to take her place. I didn't want to be the big sister. That was her job and damnit, I needed someone to protect me. She was always the strong one, the beautiful one, the perfect one in my eyes. I wanted to be like her so much and was so happy when I got kicked out of Hamilton High and was sent to Westchester High, where she was a student at the time. I got to spend one whole day with her at school before the 9/11 attacks happened the next day and we were forced to evacuate because our school was right behind LAX and there were reports that the airport would be hit next. She never returned because she got sick and found out she was pregnant and finished the 12th grade at home, or maybe she dropped out, I never really asked. In any case, the home she lived in didn't seem too bad when I got to visit. They even had a yard in the back and a nice kitchen inside. It was a house, not an apartment, and that alone was very cool to me. So, I put back on my Home Town Buffet outfit, because it was the only clothes and belongings I had there, and I braced myself to meet my new temporary family.

CHAPTER 9

AFTER WHAT SEEMED like a long ride due to LA traffic, we finally arrived at a massive, dingy, cream building with burgundy-brownish doors, shingles, and trim, in an area known as Lincoln Heights. I didn't arrive at the cute little house with the white picket fence I had imagined, or a nice family standing in the doorway wearing their church clothes and big fake smiles. I walked into what felt like a school building dressed in high ceilings and walkways, lined with doors, many doors, that led to either an office or someone's bedroom. I was checked in and processed, similar to how I was at juve, except I wasn't told to strip naked and given a uniform that signified my confinement. I was instead given a list of rules to follow, warnings of what would happen if I didn't follow them, and told with enthusiasm that I had a $100 clothing allowance and would be taken shopping later that day. Yipee. This place reminded me of juvenile hall. It felt like an institution, a school, a church, a complex of sorts, but definitely not a home. Instead of COs dressed like cops and carrying pepper spray, metal rings packed with keys and handcuffs, there were 20-plus staff who wore regular clothes, had little notepads to document our every move, and kept track of who was on their floor—similar to a teacher with an attendance list. There were case managers, therapists, social workers, life-skills coaches, drivers, cooks, janitors, floor supervisors, administrative staff, nurses, and probably a host of other staff I was unaware of. Unlike juve, where the staff all appeared to be older for the most part—at least in their 30s and above—the staff here ranged in age from young to old. Some appeared to be no older than I was. All of the younger or Black and brown staff did most of the supervision, cleaning, cooking and transporting. The white and older staff were in charge of providing us the services they deemed necessary and appropriate, like psychoanalyzing us and trying to convince us that we were capable of doing better, while refusing to address the real-life issues that got us here, and jotting down any comments or behaviors that could be used against us later in their reports. A notable difference between here and juve was that the girls walked around more freely whenever they were not restricted to their rooms, and they all wore their own clothes that were either brought from their homes, or acquired while in the group home. It's fascinating how much you can tell about someone just by looking at their clothes. Even though we were all poor, each girl tried their best to convince those around them that whatever crafty way they altered the donations that were left for us, was fashion.

On my tour of the group home, I learned there were two floors that were used to house us girls. The first floor was for kids who had children or who were pregnant, and all of the administrative offices. The second floor was for the rest of us, a mix of straight foster care kids, and others like myself, who had dual probation and dependency cases. In total, there were more than 60 of us girls and their children warehoused and living in the group home. Sixty. There was a large cafeteria in the basement that reminded me of a school cafeteria and classrooms where a few outside teachers from one of the local city or county school districts came in to teach us—or give the appearance of teaching us. The building was in terrible condition, the paint was peeling off the walls. You could smell mold in all of the bathrooms and many of the windows were boarded up or covered. You could see small fragments of glass here and there that were missed during clean-up, signifying that the window had been shattered.

When I finally made it to my room, I was blown away by how ugly and dingy it looked. It didn't look like a bedroom at all, but felt like a tiny classroom that someone shoved furniture into. The floors were tile and had the grainy print that you would see in a school classroom or front office. The doors and one wall were painted a deep, dark green, with the other walls painted a pale blue and was covered in free-hand writings and drawings from the girls who had lived there previously and were bored out of their minds whenever they were confined to their rooms. There were also pictures torn from magazines that were hanging up from the one girl who was currently occupying the space and was way too excited to see that her new roommate had arrived. I became immediately anxious when learning that I would be sharing a room with another girl, knowing that I couldn't just lie down and process all that was happening to me. I very much wanted to cry, just a little, as the realization of being detained and confined by yet another institution, disguised as a home, kicked in. I became nervous knowing that I wouldn't be able to come to terms with my new home and had to immediately put my guard up and let these girls know that I was not one to be played with. Juve taught me to strike fast and to strike first, but I hadn't planned or prepared for my introduction to this place. I thought I was walking into a home with a family, not an institution with more broken, hurt, traumatized and abused girls. I mean, I know they existed because I remembered visiting my older sister in one. But we were told that she was there because she did really bad things and was a really bad person. We never knew what those really bad things were. My sister wasn't in a gang or sold drugs to my knowledge. She didn't steal from stores like I had, or if she did, she never got caught. She was only 12 when she was detained, confined, and sent away. I wondered now how she must have felt, being so young and so alone. I at least had the privilege of four more years of life experience to prepare me for this place. I wish I had known then what I was starting to learn and understand now. I wish I knew that the letter my mother asked us to write and coached us on about how bad my sister was, contributed to a tactic to keep her away and confined, one less kid that my poor, single, suffering mother had to be responsible for. I grieved for my sister Symphony at that moment. My poor sweet pea.

Now I had to immediately decide which Charity I would give this place. The sweet, studious girl with dreams and hopes who used her mind to escape to fantasy lands with fairy dust and mermaids had already died. The weak, victim, emotional, and frail Charity was still there, buried and trying to resurface for a gasp of air every chance she could.

But no, not here. She needed to stay suppressed. She too needed to die. I needed to show that I was strong, I needed to show that this pretty face was not your punching bag, or the butt of your jokes. I wanted to be the crazy one that these girls would know not to fuck with. Pretending to be crazy, or extremely out of control, was a survival tactic many girls resorted to. Especially the ones that were too small or too big, too pretty or too ugly, too anything really that could be used against you. Crazy kept us safe, to a degree, from each other, but gave cause and justification for the staff to medicate and punish us. We were all really convinced that the other girls we were living with were scary and out to get us. We saw each other as the primary threat, we were conditioned to hate and fear each other, not the adults there, but each other. So when my new roommate, a Black girl about my height and overweight, excitedly greeted me, I stared in her face with cold eyes that were full of pain and anger for what probably felt like the longest four seconds of her life, and just blinked. I didn't say hello. I didn't want to know her name. I wasn't interested in getting to know her. I didn't want to be her friend. I turned around, looked at my bed, which at least had a six-inch mattress, an upgrade from the jail yoga mat I became accustomed to sleeping on, and sighed. On the mattress was the most hideous used cover, burgundy, with floral print that reminded me of the covers that probably doused every Black grandmother's bed. Next to the bed was an old wooden dresser that didn't match the rest of the furniture, all of which was probably donated anyway. There was a small armoire that we were to share for our clothes which, having three sisters, I immediately knew would be a problem.

Seeing that I didn't have any clothes or any belongings for that matter, the lady who was showing me around announced that it was time to go shopping. Me and another girl who just arrived that day were taken not too far away to a street populated by Mexican small businesses and reminded me of the alley in downtown LA's fashion district. Here we found discounted underwear, socks, and clothes. I was given a list of essentials to shop for: seven pairs of underwear, seven pairs of socks, two pairs of pants, four t-shirts, one bra, and a pair of tennis shoes, so long as they weren't over $20. Aside from the socks and underwear, I didn't have enough clothes to last a week, unless I wore my clothes multiple times before washing. Probably knowing this was a concern that came up often with other girls, the lady gleefully told us not to worry and that there were a lot of nice donations we could go through back at the group home. She even said one time there were name-brand items that were donated and since it was Christmas, we came at the best time. While she paid for our things, I took a moment to look around and enjoy the brief period of freedom we had. Although this wasn't my neighborhood, it felt familiar. The bustling noise of cars, horns being honked, kids walking home from school, parents waiting at the bus stop with their children, and street vendors selling everything from shaved ice, to socks. There was such a lively and far from thriving community down here, all brown people, lots of graffiti and wall art, and little old men sitting on chairs in front of their family's store having conversations that caused them to throw their heads back in laughter and display the most contagious smiles I've ever seen. Folks down here were poor, but happy. Struggling, but content. They didn't appear to be afraid of each other, or watching their backs, unless a police car rolled through. When they did roll through, everyone's demeanor changed and the look of fear overcame the smiles. Seeing the second bus roll by, I started to size up the lady taking us shopping, still having no idea who she was, or her name. She never offered the information and I didn't care to ask. I wondered if I could take her on, or if she'd catch me if I tried to run away. Freedom was calling my name, and I was tempted to just take off running. Where to, I had no idea, but I wanted to escape, I wanted to disappear. But I didn't. Instead, I grabbed the black plastic bag she handed me with my new acquired belongings, mustered the strength to say thank you, and climbed into the white county van we were transported in to go back to my new home.

When we arrived back at the group home, we stopped by one of the rooms on the first floor where a lady stood over a door that swung open at the top and stayed closed at the bottom. The lady told me her name was Anne and that I should come to her whenever I ran out of toiletries, or needed pads for my menstrual cycle. What she really should have said was that we would get one bottle of a two-in-one Suave shampoo and body wash that left a Black's girl hair feeling stringy and dry, one pack of pads, a tooth brush, a small tube of toothpaste and to make it last for a month before asking for any more. I was handed a cheap plastic basket that contained these items and a notice not to lose that either because it wouldn't be replaced, and continued on my way back to my room on the second floor. Before arriving at my room, a tall El Salvordian girl named Aileen, who could pass for another race and doused a large medical boot and crutches called out, *"What's up, girl?"* to me from the rail she was leaning on that looked over the first-floor entryway.

I couldn't tell if she was just being nice and greeting me, or if she was trying to size me up and bang on me, which was a common interaction in these institutions. When she asked me what my name was, I responded by snatching one of the crutches she was using to hold herself up and threw it over the rail. As the crutch crashed and landed on the ground below, I looked up slowly, my eyes void of emotion or care, and warned her not to ever fucking talk to me again. This little display of aggression worked for me, and people actually thought I was crazy. Hell, I was a little surprised and questioned if I actually was. The result of that episode was a mix of respect, fear and distance from the other girls inside, and forced counseling sessions and assessments with various therapists and caseworkers who were trying to diagnose what my problem was without, once again, ever asking me what was wrong. Those assessments backfired and they learned that I was extremely smart, articulate, imaginative, and deep down inside held tremendous potential. For what, none of us knew exactly, but there was definitely something there.

After making it through Christmas with cheesy gifts, well-intentioned volunteers visiting almost daily, and an outpouring of donations that definitely helped me fill in my wardrobe, things started to calm down in the group home. I quickly learned that with the visitors and volunteers no longer around and as the buzz from the holidays wore off, the home was pretty military with early-morning wake ups and a very structured day of doing a whole lot of nothing.

We were forced to go to breakfast, then school, then groups, then lunch, then activities, then counseling, then dinner, then shower, then repeat. Our attendance in all of these activities was mandatory and there were consequences if we resisted. These sessions, groups and activities were not designed to actually help us, but to impose and enforce what they felt we needed to know and how we needed to feel. They were mostly led by outside groups that would come for a few weeks, then disappear and a new group would appear. We were test dummies for all sorts of pilots and projects that opened wounds to our trauma and pain, but never closed them on the way out. We were told to speak openly about our childhood, what we felt about our families, and what we hoped for when we grew up. We were being used for research and our answers that came from emotions stemming from one of the worst times of our lives were being used to justify why these places and solutions needed to exist for us. We never saw anything of substance or value manifest from our participation, just more programs and more requirements. I learned while in here that this was a level-12 group home for girls who either had children themselves, were pregnant, or had mental health, or severe behavioral issues. I was none of those things, many of us weren't, but we were being treated like we were. I also heard they were getting paid more than $5,600 per month for each of us, which was significantly more than my mother's monthly salary, probably triple what she earned. If we had that kind of money, I wouldn't need to steal or worry about where my next meal would be coming from. I definitely wondered why my clothing allowance was only $100 if they were getting paid big bucks for me, and why this place looked so dilapidated and worn down. For $5,600 a month, I could have at least received new sheets and blankets and hair and body products that worked well on my skin and didn't leave me feeling as grimy on the outside as I felt on the inside.

I eventually dropped my crazy act and made a few friends while inside. It became exhausting and I started to lose the wherewithal to keep it up. This place was draining with all of its programming and forced group therapy. Sometimes I just wanted to sleep, or read a book of my choosing. I missed the days of going to the library on Robertson Blvd, grabbing a few books, sitting in a corner, and just reading for an hour or two. The beauty of going to the library while I was actively in a gang and selling drugs was that I knew it was the one place no one would find me, or think to look as they hung out across the street at the park. I wasn't much of a napper, but some days I needed to just close my eyes and process the events of the day. That was almost impossible here. I ended up becoming friends with Aileen, the El Salvadorian girl whose crutches I threw over the rail. She was actually pretty cool and was indeed just trying to be nice to me. I learned that she had been in foster care since she was eight years old and after being bounced around between 26 different foster homes, she eventually landed here to live out the rest of her childhood. Her mother fled El Salvador because their family was being targeted by gangs out there and like many people, she feared for their lives and came to America in hopes of a better future, in hope of the American dream they had heard about. Her mother had spent all of her money paying a coyote to help her cross the border, which he did, but not before raping her multiple times on the way there as payment for the food and water he provided her along the way. This was how Aileen was conceived, born an American and thrust into its child welfare system after her mother was deported during a raid at a downtown factory.

Then there was Blue, who was a straight-up gangsta, but as sweet as they come. Blue would walk around banging on just about everyone and would turn around the next minute and give you a hug. Blue had a round body and a round face, but she wasn't fat. She had very dark skin that she kept moisturized with a tube of vaseline, and she had the tiniest ponytail that she slicked up on the top of her head and wrapped in a blue bandana. Blue was not cute based on how we defined beauty, but she had the prettiest smile that confused the hell out of all of us because she always smiled while saying some of the most hateful things. I don't know why we clicked, but we did. She would sneak into my room at night, or swap places with my roomie, and we would talk all night about everything. Blue told me that she was repeatedly raped by her stepfather when she was little and that her mother never believed her. She joined a gang while she was in middle school because she craved family and protection, but what she got was being gang raped and passed around by them whenever they were in the mood. The rule was blood in and blood out, so she learned to deal with it until her family eventually moved away and she had an excuse to never see them again. She started only being interested in girls after that, wearing baggy clothes and bandanas to hide the voluptuous body that started blooming way too early and was the reason so many predators were after her. Blue landed in this group home because she was getting into a lot of fights at school, suspended often because no one ever asked her what was going on or what she needed. No one cared to hear the story behind her pain and her anger, they just punished her for how certain events and incidents triggered her and how she reacted to them. Like me, Blue came from probation and we bonded over our stories at juve, except hers included also being raped there by one of the COs. Apparently the one time she did divulge her history of sexual abuse in confidence and while seeking support, it was used against her and she became an easy target.

Then there was Deborah, a big and beautiful Ethiopian girl who experienced a tremendous amount of abandonment and trauma growing up and had the kindest soul. Her family emigrated from Ethiopia, but she lost her mother along the way due to illness and was bounced around from house to house with her father, until one day, he never showed up to pick her up from school. He completely disappeared and no one could find him. The authorities didn't spend any time looking for him and child protective services was called. Out of all of us, I was shocked she was here and not in a loving and caring home. She was so optimistic about life, cried often about her past, but would shrug it off and keep focusing on the dreams she had for her future about being in television and entertainment. I thought she was delirious to have such high hopes and ambitions but enjoyed hearing all of her wild and unrealistic dreams anyway. Then there was Amber, a redbone girl who had terrible acne and a few missing teeth, but you could tell that she was pretty under all of her scars and brokenness. She was 17 and had two kids, one three-month-old who stayed with her in our group home and a five-year-old who she had when she was 12 and who was in foster care at another home. Amber had also grown up in foster care and was sexually exploited and trafficked when she was just 10 years old by her foster mother's boyfriend. Amber was removed when she got pregnant shortly after her 12th birthday, but her foster parents were never arrested or punished for what they did to her. They denied it all and said she was fast and ran away often to hang out with the neighborhood boys. As soon as she left, they were gifted with new kids to exploit and abuse. She learned the hard way that those in power and positions to protect her were either the perpetrators, didn't believe her, or didn't care. Since then, Amber continued to be raped in her various foster homes until she was picked up and trafficked by a pimp who would beat her son as punishment if she failed to obey or bring home enough money. She got addicted to drugs while being exploited. It helped numb the pain and gave her a brief escape from the reality of the grown men who were pounding her, or forcing themselves into every opening on her body. She would laugh nervously and tell us that police officers would pick her up off the streets, rape her or get her to perform fellatio, then let her out with a warning that if they ever saw her out there again that meant she wanted more. They blamed her for being out there, a child. They didn't ask her if she needed help or what she was doing. They didn't see her as a child or think she was worthy of saving. They could have rescued her and her baby, but they didn't. They got their share and threw her back out to the wolves. These four girls were my group home crew and with the assistance of some of the staff who would smuggle weed in for us, we would hot box in the bathrooms, get as high as we could, and whisper stories about our childhoods and crazy experiences all night. I realized that no matter how bad I thought my story was, I had nothing on these girls.

While in the group home, I also started to get close to some of the staff. There were two staff on the day shift, Ms. Dana and Ms. Nikki, in their early 20s and best friends who got this job after applying for it together. They were kind, treated us with respect, but tried to be stern and adult-like, but we weren't buying it and made them our official home girls. We loved hearing Nikki's stories about her relationships and seeing the nice shoes and clothes she would wear to work everyday. Nikki was beautiful and we all wanted to be just like her. Dana was basic, a little mean, and wore glasses, but she was cool and kept us in check, made sure we got to our groups and activities on time, and was the lookout while we were smoking in the bathroom. Then there was Ms. Cheryl who was on the night shift. An older lady in her late 30s or early 40s, she wore a French roll just like the CO I met in juve had, but she was cool and would bring us weed and let us use her cell phone to call our boyfriends at night. Ms. Cheryl was also in foster care at one point, so she sympathized with us and tried to help in the only way she probably thought she could. We didn't give a damn what her reasoning was so long as she kept the weed and the cell phones flowing. I would use her phone often to talk to Monte and he would even come visit me on occasion. I was so lonely in there that Monte became my everything, so when I learned that he had cheated on me, my whole world came crumbling down. I called him one evening and another girl answered his phone and told me that she was his girlfriend. She told him to *"Let that bitch know who your girlfriend is,"* and he did, shattering any confidence or hope I had left for boys and their shenanigans. As payback, I started talking on the phone to different guys I had met along the way while at school or just out and about. I even talked to a few guys the girls inside would try to hook me up with, and I found little ways to restore what power I thought I had by having all of these boys butter me up over the phone and me sell them dreams about our futures together. I felt in control, but I was just bored and hurt and needed something outside of the group home's programming to pass the time.

My case manager, Dan, was a young, white and Hispanic mixed man who swore he saw something in me. During a meeting, he told me about a young lawyer's program through a Law School downtown. I was not interested in going at all, but he told me they only accepted 50 kids from the county and he selected me to go and represent the foster kids. I wasn't sure if I had a choice, but I ultimately bought into the idea when he said there would be catered lunches, and that the program was off site at the law school for a few weeks. Plus, I would get to be around other non-delinquent or foster kids, so I could pretend to be normal for a change. I entertained the idea and was introduced to the world of law where I found out I was competing with these other kids via a mock trial. One kid would be awarded a small scholarship once they graduated high school and have all of their law school fees waived if they decided to go to the law school where the program was held. College was not something I ever thought of, or had proximity to. My parents didn't really mention college to us, and although they both took a few classes at community college, they never finished. We were not raised to think that was something we had to do, this award was not only foreign but meaningless to me, so I just went along with the program. There were five groups of 10 kids and each group had a case with five students representing the defendant and five students representing the plaintiff. The case we got was a battered women's syndrome case and the role I was assigned was the attorney on the defendant's side, the defendant being the battered woman who had killed her husband. My job was to deliver the closing argument. After weeks of learning, discussing, being triggered, re-traumatized, practicing and preparing, the day finally came to perform our mock trial in front of a panel of law school students and professors. After hearing compelling arguments on both sides, it was time for me to stand up and give my closing argument in defense of this poor and helpless woman.

Before the mock trial, I had convinced my case worker that I needed something professional to wear, even if only for the last day. All of the other kids arrived dressed for the occasion everyday in their collared shirts or polos, slacks or nice skirts, even if they were only their school uniforms. I was so embarrassed by my attire that it was hard to focus and fully participate, but I sucked it up and told myself I didn't care what any of these kids thought. I was the only Black person in the whole program. Everyone else was Mexican and spoke in Spanish when they were around me, so it made it easier for me not to give a fuck. But on the day of my presentation, it was important for me to not be seen as the poor girl from the group home who they allowed into their space. Even if I sucked at the program or in my presentation, I wanted to at least feel like I belonged. My case worker agreed and $20 later, I had a cheap white uniform shirt, black uniform pants and black flats that made me feel like a million bucks at that moment. I don't remember much of what I said as I stood before the mock jury of lawyers, professors, and law students, or if I even said what I had been practicing. All I remember was being so overwhelmed with passion and grief for the woman I was defending and the choice she had to make to save herself from her abusive lover, or die trying, that I zoned out and a completely different version of myself took over to deliver the closing argument. When I came to, the panel was teary eyed and moved. Everyone just stared at me in amazement and the place fell extremely silent. Then, almost as if it were timed purposely, everyone stood up and applauded. Some shook their heads up and down in approval and others leaned over and whispered in their neighbor's ears. I was in complete disbelief, were they clapping for me? Apparently, I gave the most moving and compelling speech they had ever heard from a youth, or maybe that they had expected from someone like me. The case ended in a mistrial, which was a great outcome because we were told she would more than likely be found guilty, but to defend her the best we could anyway. Out of the 50 normal kids who were present that day, I was the one who won the award and scholarship. I was the one who defeated the odds for my fake battered client who I saw as all of the girls I interacted with at juve and in the group home. She represented their inevitable fates of violence and abuse and I defended her, humanized her, and won.

CHAPTER 10

L IKE THE BOOKS I would read, those few weeks in mock trial weren't real. They were an escape from the very real world I was living in and once that chapter was closed, it became a distant memory. I was never contacted after. I never received the award or scholarship. Maybe the group home was given additional information, but it was never communicated to me. I technically wasn't even in school, so how could I possibly reap the benefits of such an award anyhow. My 12th-grade experience was a discounted education in juve and fake school at the group home. I was probably significantly behind and had no idea how many high school credits I had, or still needed to graduate on time. Nor did I care. We didn't have a school name, a set curriculum, or received grades. We weren't taught anything really, didn't make any plans for prom or graduation. We didn't talk about life after we turned 18, except for when the Independent Living Program would come in, bribe us with a $100 gift card, and take us on the small school bus to East LA Community College to take a life-skills class. We didn't give a damn about learning how to keep our homes clean, or how to cook a meal. We were trying to survive the moment. We were trying to survive them and all of their rules and requirements and the negative words they spoke over our lives every day. We were trying to survive our emotions, thoughts of suicide, feelings of abandonment, and loneliness. We were trying to survive hopelessness. We were trying to survive each other. Give us a class on that.

The next few months consisted of mini clique wars between girls from beefing gangs, lots of arguing, fighting, being called all kind of crazy mean things by the staff, kids being medicated whenever they got too out of control, getting high, and watching girls go awol to go meet their pimps. Our group home was like a recruitment center for child sexual exploitation. There were always men lurking and driving around in cars waiting for a young girl to walk out so that he could quickly give her a ride to wherever she needed to go. Because we weren't in jail, the staff couldn't physically restrain us from leaving, but you could get in a lot of trouble if you did, especially us probation kids. If we tried to run away, we would be immediately sent back to juve, so we stayed our asses inside unless taken somewhere by the staff or if we were planning on leaving and never coming back, which also happened often. For the straight dependency kids, meaning foster kids who hadn't been to juve yet, the group home had revolving doors and they could go and come as they pleased without the threat of juve. Many of them would leave to go hang out with their boyfriends or friends if they were from a nearby community, and many would just run out after having a bad day inside looking for fresh air, or to take a walk to clear their minds. They would be lured in by attractive men in nice cars kindly offering to give them a ride, or take them for an ice cream. Soon enough, they would come back beat up and drugged up, convinced that they were in love with their captors and recruiting other gullible and lonely girls to join them. After what I learned in juve, I knew better and would never find myself walking anybody's street and selling my ass to disgusting old men for money that I couldn't even keep. No, ma'am, not I. Seeing these girls in action, I couldn't understand what they were thinking and how they could be so naive and gullible. They talked about their pimps as if they were Gods, or their saviors who rode in on golden chariots and offered them a solution to their miserable lives—and that we too could be saved from the emptiness and sadness we all were feeling. They somehow found a way to disassociate their captivity and exploitation from the perceived benefits they received in exchange. They somehow believed those benefits were desirable and they were lucky to have them. Fortunate to have a man love them, even if he beat them, or had to share him with other women, and if he embarrassed them in front of his friends and treated them like animals. For them, being worth something to someone was the prize. They felt needed and valuable. These pimps filled a void for them. They preyed on knowing that these girls had daddy issues, were empty, and just wanted to be loved and desired and of some worth to someone, anyone. We all wanted that, but I was cool on that type of love. Despite convincing myself I would never fall prey to what the streets called prostitution, another form of sexual exploitation found me and by the time it did, I wasn't prepared for the velocity at which it hit.

CHAPTER 11

ONE OF THE shows we were obsessed with at the group home was *America's Next Top Model*. We had just finished watching season one and got word that auditions were being held for season two. We would joke and talk about how we were all too short, too ugly, or too fat to ever model, but it was fun imagining it and using the hallway as our runway. We would laugh and glide down the hall just like the models on the show, or remix it and crip, or blood walk, showing off the brilliant and creative footwork that signified what side of the color line you were on. Sometimes our runway would turn into the soul train line with all of us dancing and showing off our moves, while talking shit and egging each other on. It was fun to pretend that anyone would want to turn the lens of their camera on us and make us stars that the world would drool and obsess over. Then one day, one of the staff I rarely interacted with named Ms. Shannon approached me with an opportunity. She told me she knew some people who were looking for models for a clothing catalog. I remembered seeing the Sears and JC Penney ads in the Sunday newspaper my father used to read and always wondered how those kids got in the magazines. She said it would be a cool opportunity to get away for a new activity, and that I could even get paid if I did well enough and start saving for when I turned 18 in a month.

The last time a staff member approached me about an opportunity outside of the walls of our group home, I got to pretend to be a lawyer and eat delicious catered food. So any opportunity to leave the group home I was usually open to, and to model, well, that was just the icing on the cake. I became extremely excited about this and, noticing how anxious I was to run and tell everyone and make them jealous, she quickly told me that I couldn't tell a soul. This was not an approved activity, according to her, and she was doing me a favor because she saw something special in me and only me. I felt lucky, once again, to be the chosen one from the group home to do something special and outside of our normal routine. For a minute, I started to feel like maybe I could have a chance at a normal life after all of this and modeling could be my path to get there. My mother had modeled while in Baltimore and came to Los Angeles to be a model and actress, and although those dreams weren't realized for her, I felt that maybe it would work out for me.

The staff would often get permission to take us off-site, at least once a month to spend our $100 clothing allowance. On occasion, we could convince them to take us to other places whenever they were transporting kids to see their families during home visits. We just liked to get out and if you were cool with the staff and not a flight risk, they would let some of us tag along. So when Shannon said that she got approval to take me to that special store I wanted to go in the valley to spend my allowance, I got excited, knowing that it was all a cover-up for us to go to the modeling gig instead. She told me that it would be a photo shoot and that they needed pictures to send around to other talent agents. We drove for what felt like an hour through freeways surrounded by small mountains on each side, a massive building to the left of us with a trolley carrying people up the mountain, and big beautiful trees everywhere. The tight congested neighborhood and skyscrapers I was accustomed to seeing shrinked in the background and was replaced with a skyline of houses, clean, sleek buildings, and people walking down streets for leisure, or to walk their dogs and not because it was their only mode of transportation. I only saw a homeless person or two on occasion and they were white, unlike the sea of Black and brown men, women, and children we saw camped out and living on almost every other corner in LA.

We finally pulled up in front of a beautiful, two-story home in a really nice neighborhood that was lined with trees that seemed to bend toward the top and whose branches and leaves provided a sense of covering and peace over the homes. The lawn was neatly manicured and had those fancy bushes I would only see on TV, with a cobblestone walkway and gorgeous columns at the entryway. A brown woven mat laid at the front of the door with the word "Welcome" in bright red. The front door was tall and wide and had glass in the center that you could almost see through. We could never have a door like that where I grew up. Someone was sure to break it and let themselves in. I never questioned why we were at a home and not a place of business. The thought never crossed my mind. I just felt so honored and privileged to be invited and welcomed into such a nice home that I was excited and just knew that something good was in store for me. Maybe this was God's way of saying sorry for the past two years of confinement, displacement, instability and overwhelming feeling of worthlessness I'd experienced. Maybe my being the protector and provider for others for so long was finally going to pay off and I could finally do something for myself.

When the big beautiful doors swung open, we walked in and were greeted by a tall Black man with wide shoulders, a big bald head, and very dark sunglasses. He had a small, neatly trimmed mustache and wore black slacks and a black turtleneck sweater. He had a very creepy smile and seemed pleased to see me, while shooting a look of approval over at Shannon who became giddy like a child who just brought home a report card with all A's. He introduced himself as Al, told me I looked very beautiful, and that if everything worked out today, I may be lucky enough to have him as my agent. I had no idea what an agent was or what they did, but I shyly said OK and offered a nervous smile. Shannon grabbed my shoulders, spun me around, gave me a reassuring smile, and said she'd be back to pick me up later after running a few errands.

"Wait, you're not going to stay?" I asked.

"No, you're a big girl," Shannon exclaimed. *"You got this. I'll be nearby, and just tell Al if you need anything. He's cool and I trust him, so you don't have anything to worry about. Just remember, this is a once-in-a-lifetime opportunity so don't mess it up."*

Trust him? I barely knew her and only trusted her because her job was literally to protect me and make sure I did what I needed to do and got to where I needed to go.

I immediately became nervous and something just didn't feel right, but I told myself to suck it up, and to stop being scary. So that's exactly what I did. I was just taking pictures anyway, how scary could this be?

After Shannon was let out and the doors were locked, Al walked me through the beautiful and immaculately furnished home, through a large kitchen with wide silver stoves and refrigerators that damn near touched the ceiling, to a breathtaking backyard. I had never seen a backyard like this one, nor did I know one like it existed. The yard was bordered by thin tall trees that obstructed the view of the neighbors and houses on each side. There was a large pool with what appeared to be a small cave and slide on one end of it and a jacuzzi that was running and producing the most satisfying bubbles on the other end of the pool. I imagined myself sitting in the jacuzzi while someone fanned me and fed me grapes, just like on TV. Maybe that was what the future had in store for the soon-to-be-famous model extraordinaire. On the side of the pool was a crew of white men and what looked like the setup for a photoshoot. There were cameras and wires running from the backyard into the house. There was a big, silver, shiny circle thing that reminded me of the car visor my father used to put in the window to keep the heat out of the car during extremely hot summer days. Everyone was so nice and greeted me as if I was already a famous superstar. One of the men approached me and introduced himself as Andrew, shook my hand, and told me he would be directing me through that day's shoot. He positioned me in front of one of the trees and told me to smile while he enthusiastically placed the camera over his face. Not knowing what to do, how to smile, or where to put my hands that were now serving as awkward, clunky weights, I just stood there and smiled.

"*Now, change your pose,*" he said.

"*To what?*" I asked annoyingly.

Al stepped in and told me to relax my shoulders and imagine I was hanging out laughing with friends. Pretend they were next to me and pause between every move so that Andrew could take a shot. I guess Al assumed that my teenage years were full of gossipy chatter on school benches, or at the mall hanging out with friends and oozing over cute boys, or the latest fashion and not being confined to the street, juvenile hall, and now a group foster home. I decided to channel Dione Davenport and her friends from *Clueless* and pretend I was gleefully walking through my plush private school wearing a mini pleated skirt with matching cropped blazer, laughing and tossing my head every which way. I was now keenly aware of the fact that I was still wearing the best clothes I could find from the latest pile of donations, but they seemed to love my new moves and encouraged me to keep up the good work. Very casually, Andrew told me that we needed to do a swimsuit shot and I froze.

"*Excuse me?*" I thought.

"*Yes, we are putting your portfolio together and we need multiple looks,*" he said matter of factly. Al approached me again and said not to worry, this was all a part of the process and that I'd be fine.

I said nervously, "*I don't have a swimsuit,*" feeling some relief thinking that I would be able to skip this part.

"*Don't worry, we have one for you. You're about a size small, right?*" Al proceeded to pull out a two-piece bikini suit, and

I immediately became terrified. I'd never worn a two-piece swimsuit before, let alone a bikini.

Growing up in Los Angeles, you would think all we did was swim and go to the beach all of the time, but that is so far from the truth. My aunt in Carson had a pool that we would get to swim in on occasion when we were very little, and I almost drowned in it. I recall some lady's house from church that we swam at once also, and I almost drowned there too trying to save my little sister who saw me as a life raft and staircase that she pushed under water to climb on top of to save herself. In both instances, we didn't wear swimsuits. We couldn't afford them. We wore shorts and T-shirts that became so heavy once in the water that we would stay in the shallow end to prevent from being taken under. I did finally steal my first one-piece bathing suit so that I could go swimming in middle school at a park in Cheviot Hills with my friends. I was always insecure about my body and never exposed my stomach because it wasn't as flat and tight as the girls I would see on TV. Now I not only had to wear a two-piece swimsuit but a bikini with my ass out? I started to feel really uncomfortable and was surrounded by older men who were all looking at me like vultures waiting for the main predator, my fear and anxiety, to simmer down and leave so that they could swoop in for the kill and take the rest of the self-worth and confidence I had remaining.

Al extended his arm to hand me the bikini and told me that I could change there in front of them, or go in the other room.

I gave him an annoying look of disgust, like, *"Why the hell would I change in front of you?"* and opted to go in the other room. While walking through the glass doors and back into the house, I saw the big, beautiful doors I first walked through in the distance and contemplated running the hell out of there, but where would I run to? I had no idea where I was, and we damn near crossed mountains and valleys to get there. Where the hell was Shannon? As I entered the room off the pool area, there was a young lady in there wearing a pink fluffy robe and getting ready for what appeared to be her photoshoot. She was in her 20s, white, slim, with auburn hair and a very normal-looking face. Nothing too exciting but beautiful, nonetheless. On the couch next to her were multiple outfits, all bikinis and lingerie, and she was sitting in front of a mirror gently caking on makeup, curling her eyelashes, and unrolling her hair to allow the most bouncy and gorgeous curls to flow. She stood up, smiled, and introduced herself as Montana. I very nervously said, *"Hi,"* and tried to hide how afraid I was to put on the bikini. She began to peel back her robe, revealing a pretty red lace lingerie set that left almost nothing to the imagination and complemented her red stiletto heels. I quickly looked away, shy and embarrassed, and she told me it was OK and to show her what I would be wearing. I reluctantly lifted up the two-piece bikini that was relying on the strength of my middle and index finger to keep it from falling to the ground.

She cocked her head to the side in disapproval and said, *"Well, you certainly can do better than that. Here, you can borrow one of mine,"* as she gestured toward the outfits laid out on the couch.

"I'm good," I said, *"but thank you."*

"OK, no worries. Is this your first time?" She asked.

"*Yes,*" I said, although confused by the question of it being my first time. She asked it as if I was getting ready to lose my virginity, or as if something more drastic than a photoshoot was happening. Why didn't she just ask if this was my first photoshoot, I wondered.

"*It's totally normal to be nervous and scared the first time,*" she said. "*Just pretend that you're acting, because you really are, and tap into your alter ego and it's like it's not even you, it's someone else. My alter ego is Montana, that's not my real name, you know. Montana is sexy, fierce, and ready to take on any challenge. When I leave here, I'm a student at the community college near my house, I don't wear makeup or these big curls. It's all a part of the costume. So, who's your alter ego?*"

Montana was pretty, but way too fucking chatty and talked faster than I did. Maybe she had too much coffee. I was pretty confused at that point and really wanted to say, "*Bitch, what are you talking about?*" But I instead said, "*I don't know. I'll think about it and let you know next time,*" hoping there will never be a next time. I did channel Dionne Davenport earlier, but that girl is clueless, literally, and not someone I would make my alter ego. I figured I'd just be Charity, although I was still struggling to figure out who she was. This modeling situation was causing me to question who I was. I definitely wasn't as strong as I pretended to be. I definitely wasn't in control. Who the hell was I?

I watched Montana walk out of the room and take my place by the pool. She effortlessly began to pose in various positions, commanding the camera and channeling her inner fierceness. She was standing, bending over, dropping to her knees on all fours, lying down on the ground, sitting cowgirl and looking back at the camera, back up again, smelling a rose, sticking her tongue out and licking the rim of her lip, making sexy faces. This girl had moves and was so comfortable, so graceful, and appeared to be loving every minute of it. Inspired, I tell myself to stop acting like a little bitch and get out there. If community college student Montana could do it, then certainly I could too. I quickly changed into my bikini and walked back out to the pool area. I didn't have nice hair and makeup, just a slick ponytail brushed back aggressively into a bun, but I was also only 17 years old, so I figured I didn't need all of the glam like she did.

After they finished with Montana, I was called back over, but this time instead of standing by the pool, I was asked to get in the pool.

"*Um, sir, I can't swim well and this nice bun will turn into a curly afro if it gets wet,*" I said jokingly, but being serious as hell.

"*Don't worry,*" he said, "*you're just going to stand on the stairs. Grab that floaty over there,*" pointing to the floating donut with white icing and sprinkles.

I dipped my toe in the water and shrieked, "*Oh my God, that's cold!*" But I sucked it up and continued to step in the water waist-deep after seeing the disapproving looks that darted my way. I grabbed the donut floaty device and waited for my instructions. They told me to just be natural, fun, and sexy. Play with the floaty and look toward the camera. I started off trying out some of Montana's moves, smiling first, then changing my face to serious, then my version of sexy, which didn't seem to be working. I hated my smile and the bad crown I had on a chipped tooth I got in elementary school after being hit in the face by a tether ball during an intense game with my older sister. The cheap county dental procedure I had already began deteriorating and my adult smile wasn't that pretty, at least not to me, and played a major role in my lack of self-confidence and self-esteem. I tried not to smile too much, or if I did, I smiled from my left side, which was my good side, and you didn't notice it too much.

I grabbed the floaty and put it over my head to wear around my waist and they quickly told me not to do that. Apparently, it would cover the assets they wanted to show and that I wanted badly to cover. I liked being in the water waist-deep because I felt somewhat protected, so when they asked me to step up higher, I sighed and followed directions. I was asked to grab the floaty with both hands, almost as if I was preparing to lift it up and bend over. At that moment, I recalled the one time my mother took my sisters and me to a casting call in Santa Monica for child actors. We stood in a long line for hours, dressed in our best casual clothes and our hair in nice ponytails. All of the kids, except us, had folders in their arms with photos and headshots they had taken. I recall catching a glimpse of some of the photos and they were all smiling, close-up photos, or pictures of them engaging in an activity, sport, or hobby. Lining the walls of the hallway we were waiting in were also large pictures of child stars, from Raven Symone to Jaleel White, Macaulay Culkin, and the Olsen Twins. What I recall vividly was that none of them were bent over on a donut floaty. In my head, I chucked it up to my age.

"You're almost an adult, silly, of course they wouldn't be bent over on a floaty," I thought during the mini-battle in my head with my conscience. Reluctantly, I spread my arms out,

bent over, and smiled for the camera. After what seemed like forever, I was finally finished with my photoshoot that started in the pool, but took me around the whole backyard, trying out multiple positions, backgrounds, and lighting. I later found out that the hair under my arms and sticking out of my bikini were the main reasons why we kept having to find multiple shots and backgrounds. I never shaved and was always afraid of cutting myself. Being in and out of juve and the group home where shavers weren't allowed and hairy girls were in abundance, helped me to normalize the hair on my body. As I was getting dressed and throwing back on my jeans and T-shirt, Al walked into the room to tell me I did a great job and to let me know that Shannon was on her way. I didn't see Montana again, but I did see another girl who appeared closer to my age and was having a conversation with one of the cameramen. She was dressed in lingerie and high stiletto heels, holding a cup of brown liquid, soda maybe. She was also Black, like me, with extremely high cheekbones and cat-like eyes. She wore hazel contacts and had a long flowing wig, which reminded me of Tyra Banks and *America's Next Top Model*. She must have already been a model, and she definitely looked the part. Lucky girl. I smiled at her, excited to see someone that I thought I could relate to. She looked me up and down in disapproval. This place was certainly full of disapproving eyes.

Shannon arrived, had a chat with Al in the foyer, and walked over toward me. "*I heard you were great today*," she said, "*a natural!*"

"*Really? I thought I was terrible.*"

"*No, you did great. And guess what?*"

117

"What?"

"I got approval for you to be my assistant and tag along on my weekend rides so that you can do more modeling. Now that they have your pictures, you're all ready to go."

"Really? Just like that? I can start modeling?"

"Absolutely," Al chimed in, "and in preparation for our shoot next week, I'm going to give you an advance."

"An advance? What's that?"

"I'm going to pay you early so that you can buy whatever things you need to make you look and feel good. Like clothes, makeup, and stuff for your hair."

"Oh wow, that's great. But I don't wear makeup, and I only know how to put my hair in a bun. Is that going to be ok?"

"Yes, we'll worry about all of that later. Here, we'll start you off with $500, and this is only the beginning. There is more where that came from."

My eyes lit up as I held the $500 in 20-dollar bills. I'd seen a lot of money in other people's hands when I was selling weed, but I never had this much money at once for myself. I started to immediately think of the things I would buy. Food was first on the list. I craved a double bacon cheeseburger from Tam's, but was definitely willing to settle for a Big Mac from McDonald's. The group home food was almost as bad as juve's, and I hadn't had any fast food since getting locked up the second time. Shannon said that we could stop for food, but couldn't go shopping for anything else until the day of the shoot because people would ask where I got the items from. She reminded me during the car ride as I dug into my Big Mac that I couldn't tell anyone about our secret, and I definitely couldn't let anyone know I had money. She even offered to hold it for me, but I promised her I would keep it hidden. I never paid Shannon any mind before she approached me with this opportunity. I thought it was so kind of her to think of me and want to help me succeed. I smiled the whole car ride home and started to think about my future. Maybe I could be the next Tyra Banks. Maybe I could get out of this place and just disappear into the world of Hollywood, fortune, and fame. I started to dream again. I started to believe.

CHAPTER 12

S ATURDAY COULDN'T COME fast enough. I was so excited for my next photo shoot and even started practicing runway modeling in the hallway with some of the other girls. It was easy to talk about modeling without the other girls knowing my secret because that's what we were already into. No one thought it was odd when I began to obsess over old magazines and started to care more about my hair and how I looked. Blue had some leftover reddish-orange cellophane, which was a semi-permanent hair dye, and helped me to add a little color to my hair. I didn't care about shaving because I highly doubted that I would be starting off with a swimsuit campaign, and I also couldn't shave without a shaver, so I worried about the things I actually had control over. I went through the new pile of donations and picked out any items that were half decent, or that I could alter and make cute. I really wished I had some jewelry and my nails done, but I put them on the list of things I would do with my money when Shannon took me shopping. I showered and layered on the cheap lotion we were given because I got ashy easily and borrowed some Bath and Body Works spray from Aileen. I stepped out wearing a pair of mid-thigh coral shorts and a white T-shirt that was covered in sunflowers. I wore the Chinese sandals we bought from the beauty supply that were a popular and cheap option among pretty much anyone from the hood. Mine were black with little black flowers made out of beads. I felt OK. Not great, but good enough. Besides, if this was a real campaign like the one I imagined and had been studying, they would be supplying my wardrobe and maybe even hair and makeup.

Shannon escorted me and two other girls who were being transported to visits to the ugly white van we drove around in. I didn't know the other girls, but was in a good mood, so I chatted with them, asked them about their visits, and made small talk to kill the time. Once they were dropped off, one in Boyle Heights and the other in Silverlake, we took a detour to Alvarado Street where we met up with some Hispanic guy who took a photo of me and magically produced an ID card that said I was 18 years old. Shannon said I needed it to get paid because the real producers pay with checks and Al was being nice and doing me a favor with the cash advance. I asked her why did the ID say I was 18 when I wasn't yet, and she said it was because I don't have parents who could cash my checks for me. I needed to be 18 to cash a check. That made total sense to me so I went along with it, but the ID cost me $200, a small price to pay for what's to come, according to Shannon.

After getting my ID from Alvarado Street and grabbing some delicious fruit from the vendors on the corner, we made a stop at a Ross Dress for Less. "*I know this bitch didn't bring me to no Ross,*" I said under my breath. Didn't she know Ross was the reason I was in all of this mess? I mean, it was me stealing from Ross but still, I hadn't stepped foot in a Ross ever since. "*Umm, we going to Ross?*" I asked.

"Yeah, they have cute stuff for cheap and a little bit of everything. Don't try to spend your little money all in one place. It'll be gone before you know it."

I definitely had plans on going to a mall and hitting up Forever 21, Gap, Claires, and Bath and Body Works to start, not no doggone Ross. Walking in, I could feel myself having a slight panic attack. I was extremely nervous and afraid to touch anything in there and felt as if everyone was watching me. I made sure to keep my hands out of my pockets and since I had on shorts and a T-shirt, I at least didn't look like I could stuff anything in my clothes. I followed Shannon around while she picked things out for me. I was not in the mental space to shop. This place was triggering for me and I wanted nothing more than to get out. In Shannon's hands were a bra and underwear combo, a mini skirt, and crop top. We went over to the shoe section, and I tried on a few pairs of heels that I could barely stand in, let alone walk. We settled on a pair that had a platform and gave me some ease while walking, which she assured me I wouldn't be doing much of.

"I don't like these things. I don't want to spend my money on this. What kind of photoshoot am I doing anyway? And why aren't they providing the outfits?" I wondered in my head.

I really wanted to ask her, but for some reason, I was afraid to. I was afraid that maybe she'd think I was ungrateful and would take the opportunity from me and give it to someone else. So I did what she said and ended up spending $67 on the items, which was way too much if you asked me. We left and she told me I could change once we got to the shoot, completely dismissing all of the effort I put into what I was currently wearing and the new color of my hair that you could only tell had a cellophane when the light hit it.

We drove for about 30 minutes or so and arrived at a totally different house, this one bigger and prettier than the last one. Walking through the doors, we were greeted by an enormous crystal chandelier hanging in the foyer. The space was open and flowed with no real separation of rooms by walls and doors and with very minimal furniture or art. Al walked briskly toward us, grinning like a Chester cat and thanking Shannon for dropping me off. I was starting to get frustrated with her just dropping me off. The last time she did, I ended up in a pool wearing a bikini surrounded by creepy white men. Shannon said she'd be right back. *"I have to work, you know,"* she said. Al escorted me and my Ross bag to a large room off the kitchen. I see a setup with lights, cameras, and once again, cords everywhere. There's a large bed with decorative wooden poles sprouting from each corner and bedding that had to be worth a fortune. In front of the bed was a brown leather couch with a navy throw laying across it.

"I hear you have a new outfit," Al said.

"Yes," I responded.

"Well, let's see it." I paused, remembering my outfit included a panty and bra set, so I pushed them to the side revealing only my miniskirt, crop top, and heels.

"I don't know why we got this," I said. *"But I'm fine with what I'm wearing."*

He chuckled and asked if that was it, as if he knew I was hiding the panty and bra. I told him what I had left in my bag, which he then grabbed and pulled out.

"OK, nice, this will do. Go ahead and change into the whole outfit and we'll meet you back here in five minutes."

Al left, and having no time to think about it, I quickly changed before my five minutes were up so that he didn't walk in on me half-naked.

I looked like a fast schoolgirl, the one my mother always tried to prevent me from becoming. Whenever my shorts were too short or any of my midriff was showing, my mother would have a fit. One, because she knew she didn't buy the clothes and assumed that I stole them, which on most occasions I had; and two, she also assumed I was "out there being a hoe," something she drilled into my head since I was 12 years old and contributed to the destruction of our relationship. When we moved to West LA, her daughters were going through puberty and having periods, and our neighborhood was not only filled with boys hanging out on just about every corner, but the Section 8 building we moved into was also the dope spot. The dope dealers lived in the front unit and our apartment building was one of two on the block where you could walk straight through, open the back gate, and be let out to the alley. There was a whole system for escaping cops in our neighborhood and if you were up on game, you knew which building, alleys, and cuts to slide through to make it safely to your next destination. It was rare that any of us just walked openly around the neighborhood unless you were little kids, older people, or just completely oblivious to the gang rivalry and police presence that was all around. As such, we had a lot of traffic where we laid our heads at night and our mother's method of preventing her daughters from becoming sexually active and pregnant was to preach non-existent demons out of us, tell us we were hoes if we simply and even accidentally looked toward the male species, and keep us locked in the house. We weren't allowed to play outside with our friends, go over to their houses, or walk to the park. She didn't trust anyone and if she did approve of any of our friends, their male brothers, cousins, daddies, and uncles were off-limits. I hated how that made us feel. We didn't even like boys yet, but were being accused of being promiscuous so harshly and even punished for it that we said, *"Fuck it."* If we're going to get in trouble either way, we might as well play outside with our friends until she comes home from work and sneak around the neighborhood. My mother came home at the same time every day and all of the kids in the neighborhood were afraid of her. We had a system where we would be alerted if her car was passing the block, which gave us time to run into the house before she made it down the alley and into her parking spot where Curtis, the friendly homeless man who lived in our apartment building's laundry room, would stall her. All of the kids would scatter like roaches, even though we were the only ones who were at risk of getting in trouble. My mother would have probably loved to see me standing here wearing the outfit that symbolized all of the negative words she spoke over my life, just so that she could say, *"I told you so,"* and feel vindicated in her approach. At that moment, I was my mother's worst nightmare.

Al walked in without knocking and was followed by a Hispanic cameraman and a white director named Simon.

"My, my, my, you look great," Simon said.

"Thank you," I muttered.

"Stand by the bedpost there and pose. We'll take a few shots around the room before we get started."

Al shot me a look of approval while he stood by the door with one arm folded and the other softly tugging his chin. I don't know why, but all of the nods of approval I was getting felt good. Approval was something that was foreign to me. No one seemed to approve of any of my decisions. If I got good grades in school it was good and expected, but never great. If I ditched school and sold drugs and stole from schools to survive, disapproval. If I stopped stealing from stores and selling drugs, got a job, and went to school every day, still disapproval and punishment. My performance at the mock trial was an immense and amazing feeling of approval, but was a short-lived fantasy that was never spoken of again. So to be standing in a promiscuous outfit that was far from Disney TV appropriate and to get approval was weird, but nice. I recalled the skimpy outfits the girls wore on *America's Next Top Model* and told myself this was normal and a part of the process. I disassociated myself from 17-year-old Charity and embraced the 18-year-old on my new ID card who had reddish-orange cellophane hair that came to life under the light. I walked to the bedpost and posed my little heart out.

I felt sexy and alive as I twirled around the room and started to embrace this new version of myself that I was meeting for the first time. This girl felt fierce and in control. She was loved by those who were watching and snapping photos and she felt, for the first time in her life, beautiful. She smiled with her eyes, gave sly grins with her lips, and allowed her body to flow and bend into poses that Tyra would have been proud of. During this shoot, there was a coming of age, a metamorphosis, whereby the young wannabe hood, bookworm girl that existed, evolved and transformed into the adult everyone wanted her to be. Seeing the transformation in real-time, the director walked over to Al, whispered something to him, and Al walked over to me.

"You are a star girl, just wow."

"Thank you," I said blushing. *"That felt good. I even got lost in my head for a second there."*

"Yes you did, and we loved it. Now, let's talk business," he said, motioning me to sit down on the couch. *"How would you like to make $1,000 today?"*

"A thousand dollars?!"

"Yes," he said laughing, *"a thousand dollars."*

"I would love to make a thousand dollars, obviously," I said laughing and giggling as well.

"Well, your modeling is off to a great start, but you have what it takes to be an actress."

"An actress? Really? I've always wanted to be an actress," I said, shrieking.

"Great, I'm glad we are on the same page. The director here would like you to shoot an intimate adult scene, like the ones you see on TV."

"An intimate scene? I'm not sure I know what that means."

"Have you heard of porn?"

"Porn?"

I immediately thought back to the sixth grade while living in the one-bedroom and a loft apartment we had in Hawthorne after my parents divorced. I made a new best friend, Racquel, who lived downstairs and we did just about everything together. After school, we went to our friend Ty's house, who lived next door, and Raquel pulled a VHS tape from her backpack that she found in her parents' room. Ty popped it into the VCR. The video started off with a gorgeous woman in a light pink satin robe lined with feathers answering her door and letting in the plumber who was there to unclog her pipes. One thing turned to another and the pipes he ended up unclogging were not the ones under the kitchen sink, but the one that flowed to her womb. The scene got hot and heavy with them aggressively undressing one another while passionately kissing. My 11-year-old body started to get hot and bothered, and I was afraid to take my eyes off the TV and look at Ty and Raquel. I kept watching the two now naked people in front of me and the woman, now on her knees performing acts that our little minds couldn't wrap our heads around. The look on his face was weird, as if he was in pain and moaning as if he was hurt. *"What the hell was she doing to him,"* I wondered and, *"Eww, what the hell is she doing? Gross."* The three of us immediately looked at each other, wide-eyed and scared, as if we got caught doing something wrong. The next thing we knew the two people on screen had changed positions and the woman was lying on her back as the man climbed on top of her and started thrusting his body into hers. We screamed. Racquel ran to the VCR, ejected the video, and threw it in her backpack. We went home and never spoke of it again, except when Racquel let me know that she was on punishment for a month because her parents found out when they realized that the tape had been played because we forgot to rewind it. Fortunately, Raquel took the blame and we pushed that day and that memory far back, so far that I had forgotten all about it until the word porn was said.

"Yes, I've heard of it, I'm not doing that shit though," I said, shuddering.

"*Why not? Don't you know that's how most actors get their start?*"

"*They do?*" I asked in complete shock and amazement. "*No way.*"

"*Yep, they sure do. All of your favorite actors and models have done porn at one time or another.*"

I sat back, thought about it, and became overwhelmed with what felt like such a big decision. "*I can't do it. What if someone I know sees me? What if my parents see it? My siblings? The people at church?*"

"*Listen, this one won't be played in the United States. This is for a film abroad, and you can even sign a contract saying that it won't be played here. And who cares what any of those people think? Where are they now? Remember, no one gives a fuck about you. Shannon told me your story. Aren't you in the group home because your own mother abandoned you? Who visits you there? No one. All you have is yourself and us, we are the only ones trying to help you prepare for your future. You're about to be on your own soon. Where are you going to go? How are you going to pay for it? Who's going to be waiting for you?*"

I sat back and took all of that in. Al was right. I was abandoned. Outside of the few visits I got from Monte before I realized he was cheating on me the whole time, no one came to visit me. My parents never came, no aunts and uncles, hell my extended family practically didn't exist, and I only saw them on Christmas Eve. There wasn't a nosy and in-your-business church member in sight checking on me, or praying with me. My father gave up fighting for me and all of us. The courts made it clear that Black fathers didn't matter, and he wasn't allowed to take me when my mother didn't show up to my hearing because they said he wasn't fit to have custody of me. His living conditions were not safe, and he owed too much in child support. No one was waiting for me, no one cared about what I was going through in the group home, or what I had gone through in juve and while in the streets. I was indeed all alone with no plan for when I soon aged out of the system. I guess they were all that I had. So, I said yes.

CHAPTER 13

IN FULL PREPARATION for my cooperation, in walks a 6' Black man, in his 30s, covered in layers of shea butter and body oil that brought a familiar aroma into the room and who was somewhat good-looking, but in an old man kind of way. Before he entered, Al reminded me that I was 18 years old and that's what I was to tell anyone who asked. The tall man introduced himself as Tommy and told me that I was beautiful. He took my hand, motioned me to stand, and swirled me around saying, *"Let me take a look at you."* Liking what he saw, he asked how old I was.

I puffed my chest out proudly and said *"18."*

"Mmmm," he said, *"fresh meat,"* and started to massage his groin area through the tight underwear he had on. The cameras hadn't started rolling yet, this was just him getting worked up over me. I didn't know if I should feel flattered, bothered, or scared, but I definitely felt something and I didn't like it. The director Simon called for everyone to get ready to take one, and told me to just let Tommy lead and go with the flow. There was no script or rehearsal. Simon said they wanted it to look as natural and realistic as possible, and that the only acting I needed to do was pretending that I enjoyed it, while laughing and saying he

had no doubt that I would. Before we began and while the cameras were rolling, Simon asked me to hold up my ID and state my age. I thought the ID was only so that I could cash my check, but they apparently needed me to be 18 for other reasons as well.

Take one! Simon shouted.

Tommy walked over to me, sat down on the brown leather couch, and began to run his pointer finger down my arm, stroking it ever so lightly. I looked down at his finger, he took his hand and lifted my chin up to his and started gently kissing me, pecking my cheeks first then working his way to my lips. My eyes were wide open and I stared right into his face. His eyes were closed and he was fully engulfed in his role and the character he was playing. I glanced behind him at Al, then Simon, then the cameraman who was way too close for comfort. Tommy's peck on my lips turned into a tongue that was working to pry my mouth apart. He succeeded and began swishing his tongue around my mouth while I tried my best to kiss him back, but was grossed out by the juiciness of his mouth and all of the saliva. Kissing him was different from kissing one of my boyfriends. There was no emotion or attraction to this person who five minutes ago I didn't even know existed. This man was a stranger. They all were strangers. I never closed my eyes during the kiss and held my breath while he played around in my mouth. While kissing me, he lifted my crop top and laid me down on the couch. He peeled off my mini-skirt, leaving my stiletto platform heels on. My body felt paralyzed. There were goosebumps all over and the heat from the lighting in the room and directly above my face from the camera made me feel as if I was melting and in a whole other zone. He got on his knees and began to have his way with me. A sensation shot through my body, down my spine, and into my toes. I curled them as if holding on for dear life. It hurt. I completely forgot that my enjoyment and satisfaction were the part I needed to pretend and the true acting scene. I held my breath and clenched my buttocks as tight as I could. My toes were now so curled that they looked like they were trying to burrow down into the sole of my shoe. I had one hand pushing backward into the couch and the other pushing his head back. I imagined my face screamed all of the emotions I felt because Simon yelled, "*CUT!*" I released a sigh of relief and began to unclench my body, allowing all of the tension that had accumulated to fade away. I sat up, breathing heavily, and turning my head away from all of the lights and cameras. One moment I'm lost in a zone filled with lights and sensations I never felt before, and the next I'm back to realizing that there is an audience watching and capturing this new experience firsthand.

"*Sweetie, I need you to fix your face, you're ruining the shot. Take Two!*"

I didn't want to Take Two. I wanted to take my ass back to the group home. Where the hell was Shannon? Tommy stood in front of me and pulled his underwear down.

"*Cut!*" I yelled.

Al walked over to me and I told him I couldn't do this.

"*I thought I could, but I just can't,*" I said, my eyes beginning to swell. "*I'm sorry.*"

"*It's ok, no worries. Just give me back my $500 and I'll have Shannon pick you up.*"

"*I don't have all of it. I bought the ID and the clothes and shoes. I only have like $200 left.*" I whimpered.

"I see," he said. *"Well, it looks like you have to finish because you owe me $500 and I don't like it when people owe me,"* he said, no longer looking like the nice but creepy guy I had met. He looked scary, and I was no longer sure if I was safe there. I knew enough from being in the drug game not to fuck with anyone's money, and I didn't want to find out what I was up against. My heart couldn't take yet another worry or fear at the moment. My day that started off as an exciting and hopeful dream come true, turned into a nightmare in a matter of minutes.

"You got this, baby girl. You're doing great for your first time and remember, you're doing this for your future. You need the money."

I nodded my head up and down, signaling that I understood. But I didn't understand. I didn't understand why bad things kept happening to me. Why couldn't my dreams come true without the detours and weird shit along the way? This wasn't what I signed up for. What the hell did I get myself into? I made my way back over to Tommy. He laid me back down on the couch, climbed on top of me, and proceeded to fill my body. I whimpered in pain. I closed my eyes and tried to think away the assault on my body and self-worth and pretend this was all happening to someone else. I thought of Montana and wondered if she did this too. I thought of the Black beautiful girl I saw with hazel eyes and long, beautiful wig. Was she also doing porn? When he finally stopped, my body was limp and almost lifeless, my mind completely disconnected from the body that was merely there, existing, but not in control.

CHAPTER 14

THE RIDE BACK to the group home was silent. I gazed out of the window, watching the cars speeding by and the trees standing tall and strong. While the mountains, hills, and trees faded into the background, hiding the filthy world of child and adult pornography, the skyline of the city started to appear. At least where I come from, the terror wasn't hidden behind fancy doors and picturesque neighborhoods. It was dressed in uniforms and poverty and ranged on a scale from, *"I can deal with this,"* to, *"Shit's about to get real."* I couldn't believe what I just did. I was so embarrassed, humiliated, hurt, and confused. I felt so stupid. I had spent the last year convincing myself that I was in charge and was going to hurt boys before I allowed them to hurt me, and here I was being tricked into doing porn. They played me. There was no modeling or acting career on the other side. At least not the one I thought I was signing up for. I wasn't going to be *America's Next Top Model* or grace the pages of a Sears or JC Penney catalog. I was trapped in a game that didn't play by the rules. So trapped that I would be on a new set next Saturday doing this all over again.

When Shannon arrived, I couldn't even look at her. I had put two and two together by now and realized that she was in on it. They tried to play it off as if Shannon was oblivious to what was *actually* happening when she left, and Al excitedly told her that I signed a contract agreeing to a minimum of 10 gigs with him as my agent.

"She's going to go very far. You did great with this one, Shannon," Al said, implying that I wasn't the first one they sold into this world.

I didn't respond when I heard him mention my contractual obligation. Every word he spoke was like a dagger to my soul, and I could feel every ounce of life and power escaping my body. I wanted to run, but again, where the hell would I run to? I wanted my bed and an empty room where I could scream into my pillow. Or maybe a mountain top where I could scream at the top of my lungs and curse God, and dare Him to strike me with a lightning bolt like my mother had warned if we ever used His name in vain. I thought about reporting what was happening and telling the authorities, but what authorities? The police who didn't give a shit that I was poor and stealing underwear for my little sister? The judge who kept locking me up without giving me any support or solutions? Hell, she'd probably lock me up for this, now recalling all of the girls I was in jail with who got caught selling their bodies to perverted older men. Maybe I could tell the people at the group home. Naw, they definitely wouldn't give a damn or believe me. No one ever believes us, and the place was filled with so much child sex trafficking that they were probably getting kickbacks for me too. I definitely couldn't tell my girls there. We had talked so much shit about the girls who were sneaking out to meet their pimps and swearing that we would never be dumb enough to get brainwashed into prostitution, a term that I was learning should never be applied to children and vulnerable girls like us. I would be the biggest fucking joke in there if anyone found out. I was literally trapped, and Al made sure I knew it. He threatened to make sure everyone saw the video if I didn't comply and because he got a percentage of everything I did as my agent, he told me I better not fuck with his money, while gently kissing me on the forehead.

I glanced down at my $500 handwritten check that had the name of the production company listed at the top. Al had them reimburse him the $500 I owed and I noticed he handed Shannon some cash when she returned to pick me up. I looked down at the car door handle and thought about opening it and jumping out of the car and onto the freeway. I remembered a line from the movie *The Ten Commandments* that my mother would make us watch repeatedly where Moses, still enslaved, held an old man who was dying in the mud they were using to make bricks. The old man, welcoming his fate, whispered in the softest, gut-twisting tone, *"Death is better than bondage."* At that moment, I finally knew what he meant. I looked at how fast the cars were speeding and thought if I jumped, it would probably be fast and painless. But what if it wasn't? What if I laid in agonizing pain on the freeway, broken and bleeding out, possibly being run over multiple times before all the cars finally stopped and the paramedics arrived? What if my end was hundreds of looky Lou's driving past slowly, looking at the worthless Black girl dying on the freeway, no one stopping to help, just looking, observing, maybe feeling sad, but definitely not responding to my aid? Nope, I didn't want to go out like that. So, I sat silently in the backseat, thinking and dreaming of other ways to die, all as scary and risky as the one before. Death didn't even seem simple, so life it was.

The following two Saturdays were just as bad as the first, if not worse. Their system was pretty strategic. I would be taken to cash the previous week's check the morning of the following shoot, meaning that I was stuck looking at a paper check that I couldn't spend for a week. I would then walk into different gorgeous homes owned by rich white men and shoot scenes with strange men. I would always hold up my ID saying I was 18 years old and the men would always drool over having *"fresh meat."* Fucking perverts. The things these men would do to me were beyond what my little imagination could even comprehend. I was always disgusted and horrified while trying my best to act the part. I mastered fake screaming and moaning. Sometimes it was real because it was painful, but I never embraced the pleasure. I refused to enjoy it, even when they were kind and nice to me, which they always were. The male actors had no idea that I was only 17 years old and being trafficked. They thought I was 18 and willfully there, which still to me was a problem and shouldn't have been allowed. I wondered if they had kids my age. Some of them were old enough to be my father. *"Would they find this acceptable for their daughters?"* I wondered. I was someone's daughter. Why was this acceptable for me, even if I had been 18 years old? I highly doubted the person I would be in less than a month would change from the person I was that day. So naive, so gullible, so fragile, and so broken. I wasn't thinking of my future or what any of this would mean in relation to it. My mind wasn't mature and capable of fully understanding the consequences of my actions beyond what was happening in real time, and even that was a blur. Where were all of the adults who had all of the answers and were supposed to be protecting me from myself and the bad people in this world? They were nowhere to be found. Better yet, they were the bad people, dangerous ones, the strangers my parents always told me to watch out for and avoid. We just didn't know they held the power and wore the uniforms and badges or hid in plain sight as group home staff. We thought we could trust them but it was all a lie. A big fucking lie.

I finally had enough when two assaults outside of the camera occurred. First, I was preparing to film and the director told me to come into the bathroom so that he could help me tidy up my bikini area. At this point, I still had hair down there and he demanded that he shave it off for me after I told him I didn't know how. I didn't want this man to touch me, but I clearly didn't have a choice. I went into the bathroom and he proceeded to force more than just shaving my private area. I was violated and raped and all I could do was sit there, numb and silent, until the tear sliding down my cheek solicited a reaction. *"You don't like this, baby?"* he asked after seeing the tear falling. *"Awe man, OK, I'm done,"* he said. *"Let's get back to work."*

The second time I was in a real studio and had just wrapped up the most painful scene to date with a male actor who was famous in the industry. The producer, who was a short white man with a huge pompous ego and whose arrogance was repulsive, told me to come into his office for my check, which was odd because they always gave them to Al, and then Al would hand them to me. I got into his office and he started telling me how much he loved seeing me in action. *"Let me see what else you can take,"* he said. *"Bend over on my desk."* By now, I'd stopped saying no. There was no more verbal resistance or objections, although my eyes pleaded with him not to. I was just living one day at a time, collecting my checks, and praying that the 10th scene finally arrived so that I could get out of this contract, away from Al, and away from this industry. I still didn't have a plan, didn't know where I would go, but I was saving my money and only spending it on occasion for food, clothes, nails, and to sneak shoes to my little sister who was now living in a group home not too far from mine. I would sneak out on occasion to check on her and make sure she was OK, looking to see if there were any signs of her being trafficked. She wasn't, from what I could tell, but she was being over medicated and given psychotropics whenever she acted out or threw a fit because she wanted out of there. I told myself that when I made it out, I would get my own place and take her with me. That thought is what gave me some strength to carry on, believing that it would all come to an end and peace would be waiting for the both of us.

I bent over the large oak desk stained in cherry red and waited for him to finish raping me while tears, once again, fell down and onto his desk. I stared into the puddle that was forming, grateful that the pool of tears wasn't large enough for me to see my reflection. I didn't want to see the pathetic girl in my reflection, but I did imagine myself drowning in the pool of tears. I took myself back to the two times I almost drowned, the first time accidentally floating to the deep end while attempting to see how long I could hold my breath under water. I remembered how calm and quiet it was under there. There was so much peace in the stillness of the water, not a worry or a care about a thing. Maybe water is the way I can peacefully escape this nightmare. *"Not a bad idea,"* I told myself as the producer pulled out of me and zipped up his pants. I was ready to get out of there, fuck that contract, this was going to be my last time. I had court this week and would be released soon. That would be my opportunity to rid myself of Shannon, Al, and all of these fuckers. My court hearing date couldn't come fast enough.

CHAPTER 15

THE NIGHT BEFORE my court hearing I stayed up late with Aileen, Blue, and Deborah and we made plans about how we would keep in touch after we all turned 18 and got out of there. I wondered if I would miss them and actually keep in touch. I doubted it. I was never big on friendships, and the few friends I had either let me down or were too exhausting to maintain. I always found contentment and solace in the books I would escape to. The characters were my friends and who I resonated with, and their stories and adventures were my happy place. I didn't have to worry about what they thought about me, what I was wearing, or how I looked. I didn't need to pretend to be cool or gangsta, I could just be. But I enjoyed the time I spent with these girls while here and the connection we have, even if it was just a distraction from the real shit we were going through.

While I was being sex trafficked, Blue was quietly coming out of the closet and pretending not to be gay because of the ridicule and shame she would receive from staff. Aileen was struggling with her new substance abuse problem after getting addicted to meth, thanks to a staff member smuggling it in for one of the other girls he was raping after everyone went to bed. And Deborah, as sweet and gentle as she was, was fighting the most unimaginable demons in her head—thoughts of suicide at least once a week, attempts at least once a month, and feeling unconvinced that she was meant to be happy and find joy. These were conversations and topics that we never talked about with each other. We pretended that no one knew our secrets and dismissed our problems the same way all of the adults around us had. Instead, we talked shit about the staff, how boys weren't shit, and other girls we didn't like in the group home. We got high on cheap marijuana every chance we could, and on occasion would have alcohol when it was smuggled into the group home.

Earlier that day, I met with the caseworker who steered me toward the young lawyers' opportunity. He was excited to tell me that he wrote a stellar letter of recommendation to the court on my behalf. I also met with my probation officer that day who advised that they would be recommending that my probation be terminated. I met with my social worker for all of three minutes and she mentioned something about emancipation, a big word that I never heard before and that she didn't define, but proceeded to say that I'd be 18 soon so there was no need for me to go that route. From what I could tell, my court hearing would go smoothly and I would be able to leave that damned place for good, never to be seen or heard from again. I joked with the staff I was cool with and my girls that if they didn't release me, I was going to release myself. One of the staff, Nikia, joked back and said, *"Girl, if they don't release you, I'm going to quit and help you leave."*

She was sick of seeing all of the illegal activity in the group home and how they were treating us. Nikia was only

21 years old and took this job because she wanted to help kids who were in foster care who were abused and in need of a home and loving adult connections. She thought she could be a good mentor and supporter and maybe learn a few new things along the way. What she got instead was the day shift of a facility that warehoused children for profit and treated them like commodities. She experienced a place where safety and education were just words on a piece of paper and where broken, depressed, and unloved girls went to languish before meeting their inevitable fates of homelessness, incarceration, pregnancy, and poverty once they turned 18 and were thrown out on the streets.

Poor Nikia was so ignorant, and really bought the story of a system that protects abused kids. She quickly realized that what they did was punish poor kids, Black kids and brown kids, for coming from poor and oppressed families and underserved communities. Nikia realized that most of the girls were not there because they were abused, but because they were kidnapped from their families, stripped from their mothers' arms because they didn't have enough food in their refrigerators or went to school wearing dirty clothes. The word they used to deem their parents unfit was "neglect," not abuse. Like me, no one helped them. No one offered their parents the $5,600 check they gave the group home. No one steered them toward support. Nikia learned that the girls in this level-12 group home were there because they were too old for the foster parents who wanted cute little kids, and because their reaction to their separation from their families was seen as violent and uncontrollable. Nikia also learned that Black people like herself didn't have a voice in the system. They were there to check a diversity box and to implement terrible policies under the guise of protection. Nikia, like me, wanted out. So we joked, but we were both serious as fuck.

Arriving at court the next day, I was put before the same judge for the third time, but this time I felt good. I was excited to hear what she thought of the letter from my caseworker and to hear that I won the mock trial. I stood there wearing the same outfit I wore when I delivered my award-winning closing argument and waited to hear of my release from probation and foster care. I watched her glance over the letter and look through the reports from my probation officer, social worker, and lawyer who I spoke with for less than two minutes when I arrived. I'm not sure what my court-appointed attorney wrote in their report, seeing that we never spoke since the last time I got locked up. The judge looked up at me and I braced myself for whatever question she was getting ready to ask. She had never asked me any questions directly before, but I just knew this time she would.

I had rehearsed my response and was prepared to say how sorry I was for the bad decisions I made and that I was doing so much better, even though I wasn't sorry for being poor and I wasn't doing good at all. I was prepared to show how humble I was to have received such an amazing accomplishment from such a prestigious law school and not show pride in my abilities and strengths, but gratefulness, like they want. I was prepared to let all of these fuckers pretend to be the hero in the fake story of protection, opportunity, and success that they pretended existed in their world. As the words started coming from her lips, I clasped my hands tightly together, held my breath, and only heard the words, *"I am ordering you to six more months in Booth Memorial Center."*

I died inside. She said it was for my own good, that I'd be turning 18 the next week and did not have a plan. Because of the type of group home I was in, apparently they could continue to provide me "treatment," which was complete bullshit. I was furious and yelled, *"WHAT! Are you fucking kidding me?"* Before I could start cussing her out, my lawyer shushed me and whispered that she'd put me back in juve if I had an outburst in her court. I began to cry uncontrollably as I exited the courtroom. Should I have written my own letter to let her know that I was being sex trafficked there and I NEEDED to get out NOW? Should I have written my own report about my experiences in the group home? Why hadn't anyone asked me how I was doing there? She never fucking asked me how I was doing in there! She never asked if I had a plan. Everyone knew I was turning 18. Why didn't anyone help me plan? I was completely voiceless and the words on the papers that did support my release were ignored. Was she getting paid to keep me in there? Why else would she do it? Surely, she didn't think it was in my best interest to stay in that place. Or did she? Has she ever stepped foot in a group home? If she did, they would be on their best behavior anyway. My God, how corrupt is this system?

I began to have a panic attack as all of these thoughts swirled around my head like a category five tornado. I fell in the hallway to my knees, clutching my chest, my heart feeling as if it was attempting to jump right out. I couldn't breathe. Suddenly Shannon, who happened to be my escort to court, grabbed me by the arm, told me to stop being dramatic, and walked me over to a bench where I sat and took a sip of water. No one seemed to give a damn about my panic attack. Everyone carried on, business as usual, except for the two little Black kids who were also in the hallway with their mother, waiting on an older sibling's case to be called. I looked up at Shannon, contemplating punching her in the fucking face. I needed to punch something. But I didn't. I sat up with a look of vengeance on my face and stared straight into the dingy walls of the court hallway. I realized exactly what I had to do. That night, I would run away. There was no fucking way I was showing up for my seventh filming with Al and the gang. No fucking way.

My shit was already packed because I knew, one way or another, I was out of there. Nikia stopped by and told me that she was quitting that day after hearing the outcome of my case, also in complete disbelief. We made a plan that she would quit and park her car around the corner and wait for me. I grabbed whatever I could carry, which wasn't much, and waited to hear the news. Once I received word from the other girls who were looking out, I started walking from my room which was on the far end of the second floor. I wasn't in a hurry. I took my time and with each step down the long hallway, I turned to my right and to my left, looking at every bedroom that housed at least two girls in it. I thought of the stories we shared, the pain and loneliness they all felt, and the social and emotional torture they were enduring in the group home. In a way, I felt like I was running away from my new sisters and taking a slice of their joy with me.

I got to Amanda's door and saw the residue from the flames that burned there, when one of the other girls lit an orange bandana on fire as a way of dissing her gang after Amanda stepped on an apple pie she acquired from the corner store, also a diss to the other girls' gang. I passed one of the large, boarded windows that one of the girls threw her head through after being denied a visit with her family as punishment for talking back to one of the staff. Most of the girls there didn't have mental health issues when they arrived, but they definitely acquired them while they were there, just like in juve. I guess that's how they justified placing us there. They could prove we had problems while there and after we left. I made my way down the stairs and recalled the time I threw Aileen's crutch over the rail and cringed at the thought of having to pretend to be crazy, just so people wouldn't fuck with me. I got to the foyer and saw a staff member and security guard chatting and I just kept my eyes on the door. I heard words, but could not comprehend them. It was just noise, my tunnel vision in full effect. I glanced over at them with eyes of fury, daring them to try to stop me, slowing my pace and making sure every step was met with the full intention of me liberating myself from my emotional, mental, and physical abusers. I stepped outside and immediately felt a gust of wind as it blew on to my face and felt the rays of the sun as it began to set. I closed my eyes, inhaled deeply and took it all in. No one stopped me and just like that, I was free.

CHAPTER 16

NIKIA WAS EXTREMELY kind, and I lived with her for about a week on her couch. I turned 18 while there, but I didn't feel any different. I didn't magically feel grown and ready to take on the world. I was met with the realization that I was homeless and couldn't stay there for long. Nikia's boyfriend came over way too much, and I felt like a burden on her. I could tell that she wanted the best for me, but she also wanted me to leave. I couldn't emotionally handle being kicked out, so I thanked her for all of her help and told her I would be leaving the next day. I fortunately was able to get a new chirp phone when we left with the money I had, and had a piece of paper with the phone numbers of various boys I was talking to, along with Al, Monte and my best friend Angelina's written on it. I didn't have a plan at all and didn't know who to turn to. I thought about calling my mom and begging her to take me in, but instead of taking me in she would more than likely turn me in, so that wasn't an option. I started messaging a few of my exes or boys who I was talking with to pass the time in the group home, praying that one of them would offer to come to my rescue. I hated asking anyone for help, so I didn't. I refused to ask anyone for anything. I didn't want to owe anyone, but if they offered, I wouldn't say no. I spent the next day in a McDonald's, then a library so that I could use their outlet to keep my phone charged. I spent a full day talking and catching up with one ex and another guy I had been speaking to before I started doing videos. Neither of them offered to take me in for the night and allow me to sleep on their couches until I figured things out. I told them I was homeless and needed somewhere to crash. They sympathized, felt bad, but didn't offer to help me. That night after the library closed, I was all alone with nowhere to go. I walked to a small park that was nestled between a few apartment buildings in Hawthorne, not too far from where Nikia lived and the library I was in most of the day, and sat on a bench furthest from the park lights. I was immediately hit with the realization that I was alone, cold, homeless and scared—very scared. I was overcome with embarrassment for sitting on the park bench, knowing that I would be sleeping there if no one came to my rescue that night.

It started to get colder and colder, and I didn't have a blanket. I didn't think to buy one earlier because I had no idea I would have to succumb to sleeping on a park bench. I reached into my backpack and began to put on as many layers of clothes as I could. I looked silly, just like all of the homeless people I would see when passing by in the cars or buses. I now understood that despite the deep poverty I had experienced and grew up in, we still had privileges others didn't have, which was sad in and of itself. After hours of sitting there, layered in clothing and still freezing cold, I tried my best not to fall asleep. I was afraid someone might rob me, rape me, or kill me. I needed to stay alert. I had nothing to protect myself, only my phone. I began to cry, harder than I ever had before.

I was grieving the situation I found myself in. Grieving the need to run away from my group home so that the weekly torture could stop. Grieving the childhood I was robbed of. Grieving the way people who claimed they were punishing, criminalizing, and fostering me for my own good did nothing but cause me more harm, agony, and pain. Grieving how I was deceived into doing porn and my dreams, hopes, aspirations, and trust in people were completely demolished. I grieved the loneliness I felt, the lack of support I had, and the fact that no one in that moment gave a damn about me. The cold I felt that night was debilitating, like swords being stuck into my spine. I was afraid to move positions because the sting of the cold would send throbbing aches throughout my whole body. I yearned for the thin yoga mat I slept on in juve and would do anything to not have to ever sleep on a cold park bench again. I was afraid to close my eyes, because if I did, I wasn't sure if I would wake back up. But what did I have to wake up to? Absolutely nothing. So I allowed sleep to take over and the cold to consume me. Not waking up wouldn't be so bad, that is actually the moment I had been waiting for. A seemingly painless death, in my sleep. God must be out there after all.

The next morning, I woke to pigeons tearing through my bags. After shooing them away, I sat back, disappointed that death didn't pay me a visit after all. I gathered my belongings and started walking back to the McDonalds. I was starving, but trying to save as much of the money I had. When I left, I had close to $1,000 in cash saved after spending more than I should have on myself and the girls inside. I would buy us fast food, clothes from one of the cheap fashion stores the staff took us to whenever the $100 they gave us ran out, and other random things I didn't need. Buying things was therapeutic to me, no matter how small, cheap, or insignificant the item was. The act of spending my own money and not having to ask for permission was an act of power to me. But my $1,000 was running out. I offered Nikia $500 for letting me stay with her and because I was eating her food, taking baths, and taking up space. She accepted it, which I hoped she wouldn't, but she did, so I was down to $500. I thought about getting a motel room, but I didn't have an ID after throwing away the fake one. I couldn't go get one because I ran away from my group home, and Nikia told me that I more than likely had a warrant out for my arrest. Going to the DMV to get an ID would send me right back to jail, and that wasn't an option.

I figured I would live off of the $500 until it ran out, relying on 99-cent cheeseburgers from McDonald's and hotdogs from the 7 Eleven. Surprisingly one of the guys I was talking to, Brandon, messaged me and asked if I wanted to hang out later. I immediately got excited because I knew that meant I would at the very least get to sit in his car, or the apartment he was living in with his parents. But I looked a mess and probably smelled just as bad. I didn't have any toiletries on me and I was using all of the stuff Nikia had in her bathroom when I was living on her couch. I was dirty, smelly, and my breath was rank. I ran to Big Lots down the street when it opened and bought their cheapest toothpaste, tooth brush, deodorant, and soap. I even found a pack of clean underwear, a hairbrush, and a small container of pro-style hair gel. They didn't have a public restroom, so I had to walk back to Mcdonald's and use their restroom to clean up, brush my teeth, and brush my hair. The Rocawear jeans I borrowed from Nikia when I was oozing over her wardrobe and promised I would return one day were still looking good and my shirt was clean, so I felt OK about what I was wearing. The last thing I needed was to be turned away by someone I was praying would provide me shelter, simply because I looked a hot mess and smelled like I hadn't showered.

When Brandon finally arrived after what felt like the whole day, we hung out in his car, talked, smoked weed, and he invited me up to his apartment. It was getting late and I was desperate to have somewhere to sleep that night so I slept with him, although I didn't like him and wasn't attracted to him like that. Being intimate with him meant that I was guaranteed a warm bed and possibly a shower in the morning. I repeated this for the next week with him and my ex, Monte, who I reluctantly started talking to again. I managed to spend a night at Monte's cousin's house again when Brandon had to take a break because his parents were starting to complain about me being there too much. After both Brandon and Monte went ghost on me for a few days, I spent the night in a complete stranger's car after offering the last $100 I had. They felt sorry for me and took the risk of letting me sleep there because they were poor and in desperate need of the $100 I offered.

I made the decision out of pure desperation to call Al, my trafficker. My money had run out, I couldn't get a job without an ID. I tried. I was terrified of stealing food or acting out my thoughts of suicide. I called the one person who I knew I could get money from in exchange for the only thing I had of value in this world, my body.

Al sounded happy to hear from me and came riding in on his black chariot, thinking he was my calvary. When he arrived his tone and energy was off and he was different—meaner and angry with me.

"Girl, don't you know how much money you cost me? Why did you run away like that? Haven't I been good to you?"

"I'm sorry. I wasn't running from you, I promise. I was running from the group home," I replied, *"and I just finally got a phone and was able to call you."*

He pretended to buy my story and realizing how desperate I was, he told me he would get me a room and that we had a lot of making up to do, but he would fix everything. That night, he got me a room at one of the nicer motels in the valley, and I was finally able to have a good night's sleep and a shower without anyone else there. I didn't have to worry about tossing and turning too much and waking up whoever was sleeping next to me, or having to sneak to the bathroom in the middle of the night, scared that someone's mama or cousin would hear me and not want me there because I accidentally woke them up. I didn't have to cross my fingers and hope I was offered a shower, which only happened once. I was able to shower as long as I wanted without any time limits or restrictions like in juve, the group home, or while at the bequest of someone's charity. I woke up the next morning feeling better than I had the last few weeks. There was peace in having something to myself and being alone, even if it was only in a motel room.

I stood in front of the bathroom mirror and saw how horrible I looked: defeated, dehydrated, the look of misery stained on my face, and just a hot-ass mess. No wonder Brandon and Monte were ghosting me. I spent time fixing myself up as best as I could with the remaining toiletries I had left. The motel offered cheap shampoo and soap, which made my hair feel stringy, but at least it was getting cleaned. All of my clothes were dirty, I hadn't washed any of them since I left the group home. I messaged Al and asked if he could take me to wash my clothes and he told me not to worry about it. He arrived with a bag full of women's clothes and lingerie for me to choose from that were used, probably left over from sets, but they were clean. I picked out the items that would fit and that weren't too skimpy and changed in the bathroom. Al said we had a big day ahead of us and that we needed to get an early start.

After grabbing breakfast burritos from Carl's Jr., he took me to a little clinic where I had to get tested for HIV and STDs. We never did this before, and after reading through a few of the pamphlets in the waiting room, I became terrified at the possibility of having a serious disease or infection. I used protection with Brandon, but not with Monte. The nurse pricked me with a few needles and drew some blood. They had rapid tests to let you know right away if you had something and fortunately, I was clean and given a letter saying such. That day, I would have my first threesome with two men. I couldn't bury my face into a pillow this time or take small moments to hide and escape from the shame of the moment. These men were aggressive and fed off of my terror. They could tell I was scared, and they liked it. They made me do things simply because they got off on it being my first time and my being so young. They felt powerful and in control. They *were* powerful and in control. That week I would experience many firsts with both girls and men, some of whom were the most famous and popular in the industry. One of them forcibly encouraged me to hang out with him after, going first to his apartment, shopping for a nice dress and heels, then to a warehouse in downtown LA.

We arrived at the warehouse in the middle of nowhere surrounded by industrial buildings. Many of the buildings looked vacant and inoperable, with busted windows and vagrants loitering around. A black gate opened and suddenly there were nice cars everywhere, parked in three straight lines and managed by a valet attendant. We got out of his car, walked up a long flight of stairs, and entered a heavy metal door after being wanded down and checked by the bouncer at the front door. The actor held my hand while we walked through the darkness of the space and down a long corridor. There were lights coming from various rooms. To the right, women were fixing their makeup and hair, some showering and walking around naked. To my left, the men were doing the same. Further down, there was a vast open space with tables covered in silk linen. Poles were coming from the ground and extending into the high ceiling, with exotic dancers softly and gracefully wrapping their bodies around the poles in various directions, climbing up and sliding down, some wearing only a barely visible thong.

There was a bar to the left of us and he instructed me to sit at one of the tables while he grabbed us a drink. I sat, looked around, and realized that this place was a cleverly structured maze of sorts, with doorless rooms, nooks and hallways that twisted and turned. The lighting was extremely low and, in some places, completely absent. Soft classical music played throughout the space. He returned with two drinks, both whisky straight, that I began to gulp down quickly just like I did before every filming to calm my nerves and numb some of the pain. He gently put his hand on top of mine and said, "S*ip it slowly, like a lady.*" I obeyed. He proceeded to take me by the hand again, leading me toward the other dark hallway with the doorless rooms. As we passed them, various scenes of intimacy were on display—but not because an adult film was being produced. They were all having wild, passionate, uninhibited sex for pleasure. There were rooms with themes, like masks and feathers, and there were rooms that were completely dark and you had no idea who you were kissing or being intimate with. You were unseen, but touched, unrecognizable, but desired. The sick beauty of it all was that as I slowly walked through each room and watched in awe, I was able to say no when people approached me or groped at me in the dark, and they listened. They respected my no and didn't force me to do anything. For the first time and in the weirdest most sexual place I've ever experienced, no meant no. What a relief.

The night ended with me experiencing sex on a whole other level without having to physically engage in it. Sex to me was always something that benefited the boy or the man and that we did for their sake and not our own. Sex was a chore and an activity that was often forced or taken. It was something you did so that the person you wanted to love or like you, kept you around. It was the only thing of value you possessed, unless you were blessed with beauty as well, but even that was relative to the person experiencing it. I witnessed sex that night that both the men and women enjoyed. It was consensual, pleasurable, and fun.

CHAPTER 17

THE NIGHT I observed consensual and pleasurable sex, Al also had a fit that I went out with the famous adult film star. He felt threatened and worried that someone else might take me from him, as if I belonged to him. Al was holding the majority of my checks until I fulfilled my contractual obligation to punish me for running away and not calling him. He paid for my motel rooms and made sure I had food and clean clothes, but only gave me a fraction of what I earned. What he did provide he made sure I knew would be deducted from what he owed me. That day happened to be the same day I fulfilled my contractual obligation, but he refused to give me my money, saying he had another opportunity that he needed me for. There was no way in hell that I was selling my soul to this devil again, and it didn't sound like he was giving me a choice. I had been in contact with my older sister who was now living in north Long Beach, and she was going to let me stay on her couch for a while in the small apartment she lived in with her husband and my niece. I started making plans on my own and figuring out my next step.

When it was clear that Al was playing me, I ran away in the middle of the night with the little money I had. Al called my phone incessantly, left threatening messages, and vowed to find and kill me. I was scared, but content with my decision. There was no winning in that life for me, no opportunity, and not even the money I was promised. I felt safe with my sister, even though she didn't know my secret. I also knew she couldn't help me for long, seeing that she and her husband were also struggling and barely making ends meet. Monte came back around and said he would take care of me. I forgave him for cheating. He bought me meals, gave me rides, and also got me pregnant. There was no way I was having a baby, let alone his baby. There was no way I was bringing a child into this world to potentially experience the things I had experienced. Who was I to bring life into this world so that they could suffer, deal with poverty, and be in a constant state of survival? I didn't have the heart to do that. But Monte, he wanted the baby, and insisted we keep it.

He introduced me to his mother and sister for the first time the day I told him I was pregnant, and they invited me to come live with them. I was so confused and unsure of what to do. I had not only Monte but his family wanting my baby and wanting me. They were excited and I couldn't comprehend how anyone could want me, let alone my unborn child. When I made the scariest decision of my life to keep the baby, I knew that I couldn't peacefully have this child with a warrant out for my arrest. What if I got caught halfway through my pregnancy and gave birth while in jail like Espinoza had, handcuffed to my county hospital bed, my baby torn from my arms after barely being able to hold and smell it, and put into foster care? What if I got arrested after giving birth and we both had to suffer the agonizing pain of being separated, unsure of either of our fates and if we'd ever be reunited again? I couldn't do that to my baby. I finally had something to live for, someone who would love and need me, and that was the best feeling I had ever experienced.

I went to a friendly cop near my sister's house who would often drive down the alley where her apartment was to visit his girlfriend that lived in the building. I asked if he would look me up in his system to see if I actually had a warrant and make sure that I wasn't overreacting for nothing. I indeed had a no-bail warrant out for my arrest. He assured me that because I was a minor when the warrant was issued, that if I turned myself in, I would only do a night in the police station because the reason for my warrant was extremely minor, according to him. He proudly turned me in, probably meeting his quota for arrests that day, and I was booked at the Long Beach Police Department. After being processed, I didn't spend the night in the police station like I had hoped. I was instead transported to Lynwood Jail where I spent the night and would be transported to court in the morning. I was given an all-white prison uniform with black letters that read "LA County Jail," and housed in a cell by myself. I could see other women being transported back and forth, walking in lines similar to how we had in juve, but they were all chained at the wrist and ankle. I didn't speak to anyone, and no one spoke to me. The facilities were in terrible condition and the incarcerated women were tasked with keeping them clean. Lynwood Jail was the first time I saw actual bars as doors, just like on TV or on "WANTED" posters. Being locked inside of a cage with bars made me feel primal, animalistic, angry, and dizzy. I wondered if it was by design that we were to internalize inferiority and brace ourselves for guilt by default because of who we were and where we came from. Those bars made me question why I ran away, and I felt in trouble for doing so. The cops at the police station didn't take my statement, they didn't ask me why I left, or how I was doing. They didn't care about my story, only the charge associated with the offense and the tally next to their names on a board that represented how many of *us* they were able to take off the streets.

The following morning, I was transported on a large silver and black bus with a white stripe across both sides that read "County of Los Angeles Sheriff's Department" in bold black letters. I would see these buses from time to time and always wondered who was on them. You could never see inside of them, the windows were tinted pitch black and were always extremely high up. Now sitting on one, something I never would have imagined, I looked out the pitch-black window as it glided down the 110 Freeway in the carpool lane. I looked into all of the cars we passed and stared at the people in them. Free people. I just wanted to be free, like them. I just wanted to live, have my baby, raise my baby, and protect my baby. I prayed that I got a judge who would do the right thing, show some compassion and order support that would actually help me. I hoped that anyone would ask me if I was ok and that this time I would be allowed to speak and have a voice. When we exited the freeway and made the final left turn, my heart dropped. We were back at Eastlake Juvenile Hall and I had to appear before the same judge, for the fourth time. She was upset that I had run away and disappointed that I wasn't grateful for the additional six months she gave me in the group home. Had she ever asked me a question directly, she would have known why. But she didn't then, and she didn't now. As punishment, she ordered me to serve three weeks—21 fucking days—in LA County Jail. I truly hated her.

Juve was daycare compared to county jail. I was transported to the Twin Towers Correctional Facility in Downtown LA, which was a huge complex with no visible bars from the outside and nestled neatly between warehouses, businesses, chronic homelessness, and train tracks. I waited in a large, cold holding cell that had a single concrete bench for hours before being processed. There were more than 20 of us packed into one small space and I, like the majority of the women there, alternated from sitting on the cold floor, to standing, to eventually laying on the floor. We weren't given any food or water, and we did not have access to a toilet. Some women urinated on themselves, others were having severe withdrawal symptoms while coming down from whatever drugs they were on. Many of the women were struggling with some kind of mental health issue, and some were clearly picked up for prostitution and still wearing the revealing outfit from the night before. All of us were Black and brown, poor, and trying to survive as best we could. When it was finally my turn to be processed along with a handful of other women, we were taken into another cold room, told to strip naked, squat, and cough. In juve we were never forced to be naked in the room with other girls. Although there wasn't much privacy during shower time, we at least had a sliver of control over how we navigated the tiny towel that was covering us, that we quickly hung up after stepping in.

After confirming none of us were smuggling in drugs or other contraband through our vaginas, the guards gave us a liquid to rub all over our bodies and sprayed us down with a high-pressure liquid that sprouted from what looked like a thin metal hose. It didn't appear to be only water, but some kind of chemical or cleaning agent that left my sensitive skin feeling as if it were on fire. Next was the infirmary for our medical exam and assessment. We were pricked with multiple needles and given multiple shots, vaccinations I imagined, although we were never asked if we already had them and never informed of what we were being injected with. They asked if I had any diseases that I was aware of and if I was pregnant. I said no to both, having already made up my mind before arriving that I would not tell a soul about my pregnancy. It was imperative that I kept it a secret so that my unborn child would not be weaponized against me and used to threaten me into submission, of any kind. I also feared that someone may try to take him from me, kick me in the stomach, or cause me to miscarry him, like many of the horror stories that I heard about. I was going to guard him and my secret with my life, do my time, and get out of there. I was given a white wrist band to wear that indicated the type of offense I was locked up for. White, ironically, being associated with the lowest level of threat. After leaving the infirmary and after hours of not eating or drinking, we were handed a brown paper bag that had a piece of fruit and a soggy sandwich in it, which I devoured. Arriving at the pod I would be housed in, I was shocked to see how chaotic the place was. In addition to the pod being lined with dozens of metal cells, there were also bunk beds in the middle, triple-stacked bunk beds to be exact, and more women than could fit in the space we were being forced to occupy. By the time we arrived at the pod, it was 2 a.m. and the place was dead silent. I was ordered to sleep in the middle bed of the only available bunk and nervously climbed in, afraid of stepping on the woman's bunk below, or touching the one above. The guards left me, and I curled up and embraced the sleep, too exhausted to be scared, too tired to check my surroundings, too worn out to care. I just slept and allowed my sorrows of the day to be absorbed by the now even thinner yoga mat I was sleeping on, so thin that I could feel the coldness of the metal bed frame under it.

In less than four hours we were all awakened by a loud bell and bright lights. It was time to get up and face the music. Hopping out of my bed, I looked down at the jumpsuit I was given only a few hours ago and that I hadn't paid much attention to because I was extremely tired. I rubbed my hands slowly down the bright orange uniform and looked up at the sea of eyes that were observing me, with a rainbow of wristbands that indicated who I should watch out for or be the most afraid of. I became nervous and unsure of how to show up in this space. This place was different. The people were grown and many of them looked like the world had kicked their asses ten times over. I was also fatigued from not having enough food or sleep and being pregnant, so I just stood there, with no emotion, nor physical or verbal response or reaction to my surroundings. I hoped no one fucked with me, but I was too weak to do something if they had. I just existed as a moment in time, hoping for the best, but expecting the worst.

I learned that day that my bunk mates who were both wearing blue wristbands were both locked up for murder, and I was incarcerated during a time where our county was experiencing severe overcrowding in its jails and prisons. The women in the pod were not what I expected at all. They were not vicious animals or violent people, although some of them had committed violence out of survival. They were kind to me and treated me like I was their daughter or sister. Many of these women were someone's mother and had children they yearned to be with everyday. Because I was the youngest and baby in the group, they looked over me and protected me, braided my hair, and shared their stories with me in an effort to warn me of the horrors that existed in the world, unaware that I had my own horror stories. These women were the direct manifestation of our society's unwillingness to address racism, poverty, inequality, and inequity and the many ways in which oppression existed and intersected across communities, gender, race, socioeconomic status, inability, and lack of opportunity. Many of them had stories of experiencing the foster care and juvenile justice systems like me, and once they aged out, were only met with more poverty and homelessness. They experienced abuse, domestic violence, more sexual assaults by friends, family members and strangers than I could keep up with. They were raped and assaulted in just about every institution they were put in by fellow prisoners and staff. They were introduced to drugs at a young age and were the consequence of our country's criminalization and punishment of a public health crisis— the crack epidemic—that turned into a war on drugs, which meant a war on Black, brown, and poor people, and mass incarceration. These women made mistakes and did things they deeply regretted out of survival or because they suffered from unaddressed mental health issues. Some of them were locked up for unsuccessfully trying to kill themselves and end the mental and physical torture and confinement this world offered them. When they failed, they weren't offered treatment, they were offered prison.

Many of the guards there were criminals. They beat the women for the slightest provocation and put them in solitary confinement for infractions as small as looking at them the wrong way. Women were raped by both female and male guards, and even impregnated. Some women were killed by medical neglect. Pepper spray filled the air at least once a day. Our names, for the most part, weren't our last names that we were to be identified by, but instead "monkey bitches" from guards both white, Hispanic and Black. Internalized racism and bias amongst the guards that were Black or of color was rampant, as they tried their hardest to disassociate themselves from the Black and brown people society rejected. Treating us badly made them feel equal to their peers and proved to white and powerful people that they weren't like *us*. Little did they know that as hard as they tried to not be "that nigga," they would always be seen as such. I kept my head down, followed the rules, and read books the whole time. One of those books was *The Coldest Winter Ever* by Sister Souljah and the main character, Winter Santiaga, became my imaginary best friend. Together, we both went through an extraordinary life change at the age of 16 and found ourselves in the most terrifying and horrific situations. We both were survivors. Her story made me feel as if I wasn't all alone and someone understood my pain.

After 21 days of cold showers, terrible food, witnessing countless fights and arguments, and experiencing guards treating us like the scum of the earth, I was finally released. I was told there would be no more probation, court dates or being confined to institutions, so long as I didn't get into any more trouble. Just like that, they let me go, almost as if nothing happened and didn't ask if I had a job or somewhere to live. They opened the big iron doors on an 18-year-old girl who they knew was in foster care before running away and closed the door behind me without a concern about how I would fare, or if they were dumping me into a situation that would ultimately land me back in jail. I wasn't given bus fare or a phone call, I was just kicked to the curb. Standing outside of the walls of the Twin Tower County Jail holding a clear plastic bag with the few belongings I had on me during my arrest, I allowed the rays from the sun to fall sharply on my face as I closed my eyes and absorbed my freedom. Lowering my head, I looked into the distance at the bustling city, smog-filled skies, and lack of opportunity waiting for me. I recounted in my mind the stories of the women inside and how they battled poverty, homelessness, sexual exploitation, abuse and incarceration. I knew that I too would continue to experience some of those things, but I made the decision to refuse to let the stereotype and statistics of young Black women like me be my destiny. I knew no one would question why I succumbed to the pits of shame, failure, and defeat. People like me were expected to be nothing and do nothing, and to remain inferior so that others could continue their superiority and profit off of our oppression and poverty.

I had no idea how I was going to do it, but I decided then and there that I would love my child as an act of resistance.

I would live as an act of resistance. I would become someone in this world as an act of resistance. Resisting all that I was told I could not have, or could never be. Resisting being told that I was worthless and would never amount to anything. Resisting not having a voice and those in power dictating my fate. Resisting believing that the policies and people in power were there to protect me and support me. Understanding that they were the real strangers who possessed a danger like no other. I badly wanted to confront all of the individuals who played roles in the systemic oppression and pain I experienced and tell them to wake up and snap out of it. The judge who only judged, but didn't care to see or hear me. The COs who felt righteous with their uniforms, handcuffs, pepper spray, and chains. The group home staff who were complacent and complicit in their roles, exploiting the children they knew no one was checking on or cared for. All of them colluded with the social conditioning and devaluing of our most vulnerable populations of children, women, and men. They are actors in systems that breed generations of people that will either have systems forced on them through incarceration and foster care, or become reliant on them through welfare and other social services to respond to our society's inability to invest in prevention and the true healing our communities need. Why couldn't they see that they were being used? How could they get so comfortable that even their own biases continued to perpetuate the harm and oppression? I made a vow that my unborn child deserved and would get a life better than what this life offered me. All of these strangers created something in me they hadn't planned for, something they wouldn't be ready for, and someone that they would never see coming. I would be a force of truth, accountability, and real justice that would be their worst nightmare in the future. So strangers, beware: Your "super predator" just may become her community's superhero.

ABOUT THE AUTHOR

CHARITY CHANDLER-COLE IS a fierce expert and advocate for children and families impacted by child sexual exploitation, and the foster care and juvenile justice systems. As a sought-after speaker and social-justice activist, Charity uses her many platforms and voice to influence and impact social structures, policies, and systems that have negatively and disproportionately impacted and oppressed vulnerable communities and people.

Charity serves as the CEO of CASA of Los Angeles, Court Appointed Special Advocates for youth impacted by the foster care and juvenile justice systems. In addition to filling this significant leadership role, Charity serves as commissioner with LA County Children & Families, where she is co-chair of its Racial Justice Committee. She sits on the African American Advisory Board to District Attorney George Gascon. Charity was a founding board member of the Anti-Recidivism Coalition (ARC), serving eight years on the board for the non-profit that works to end mass incarceration in California.

Charity is completing her doctorate degree in educational leadership for social justice at her alma mater, Loyola Marymount University. She is a wife and mother to four beautiful children and was, until recently, a relative caregiver and legal guardian to her nephew for more than 11 years.

Having harshly experienced both the juvenile justice and foster care systems as an adolescent, Charity uses her powerful story of redemption and triumph to inspire people under the mantra, *"If Charity can do it, then so can I."*

https://www.charitychandlercole.com/

RESOURCES

Commercial Sexual Exploitation of Children (CSEC) aka, child sex trafficking, is a crime and involves a range of crimes and activities involving the sexual abuse or exploitation of a child under the age of 18 years old, for or in exchange for anything of value such as money, housing, food, drugs, protection, etc. Examples of crimes and acts that constitute CSEC include:

- child sex trafficking—there is no such thing as a child prostitute!
- child sex tourism involving commercial sexual activity;
- commercial production of child pornography;
- online transmission of live video of a child engaged in sexual activity in exchange for anything of value.

If you or someone you know have been a victim of child sex trafficking, below are a few resources for support.

Los Angeles/California Organizations

- Alliance for Children's Rights: https://allianceforchildrensrights.org/

- Children's Law Center (CLC): clccal.org
- Coalition to Abolish Slavery and Trafficking (CAST): https://www.castla.org/
- Court Appointed Special Advocates of Los Angeles (CASA): https://casala.org/
- Saving Innocence: https://savinginnocence.org/

NATIONAL ORGANIZATIONS

- <u>Court Appointed Special Advocates (CASA) https://nationalcasagal.org/</u>
- <u>National Center for Missing and Exploited Children (NCMEC): https://www.missingkids.org/home</u>

Educate yourself!

Here are a few of Charity's favorite books
and authors relevant to this work.
The New Jim Crow by Michele Alexander
Slavery by Another Name by Douglas A. Blackmon
A Piece of Cake by Cupcake Brown
Shattered Bonds and *Torn Apart* by Dorothy Roberts
The Color of Law by Richard Rothstein

Printed in the USA
CPSIA information can be obtained
at www.ICGtesting.com
JSHW060750100923
48071JS00007B/7